COMICS REBUBBLED

Writers
Kim Fuller
Paul Alexander

Additional material
Paul Henry

Designer
Mark Reeve

Production
Sophie Gibson

Illustration
Imogen Tooth

Comics Rebubbled acknowledges these
fantastic artists of the Golden Age and
the Silver Age of comics

Bill Everett
Jim Aparo
Pat Boyette
George W Trendle
Al Williamson
Fran Striker
James Jewell
Mike Sekowsky
Joe Sinott

Publisher
Comedyplaza Publishing

This comic is
available online at
comicsrebubbled.com

Printer
Pureprint

WE'D JUST BEEN THROUGH THE PANDEMIC, ZOOM CLASSES AT UNI HAD BEEN A TOTAL WASTE OF TIME AND I'D LEARNT FUCK ALL. I WAS ABOUT AS EQUIPPED FOR FINDING A JOB AS A THREE-LEGGED GERBIL WAS FOR HUNTING WILDEBEEST.

BUT THERE WAS AN UPSIDE: I WAS YOUNG, BLONDE, HOT AND MY MUM COULDN'T CONTROL ME. I WAS THE CROTCH-ROCKET OF THE BAD BIKER BOYS OF THE TOWN AND MOST OF THE TIME...

I was Stoned and Shit-faced!

LAVERNE – GET IN THE SHACK NOW OR YOU'RE GROUNDED!

PART 1

DO I LOOK LIKE I GIVE A TOSS? HAHA!

3

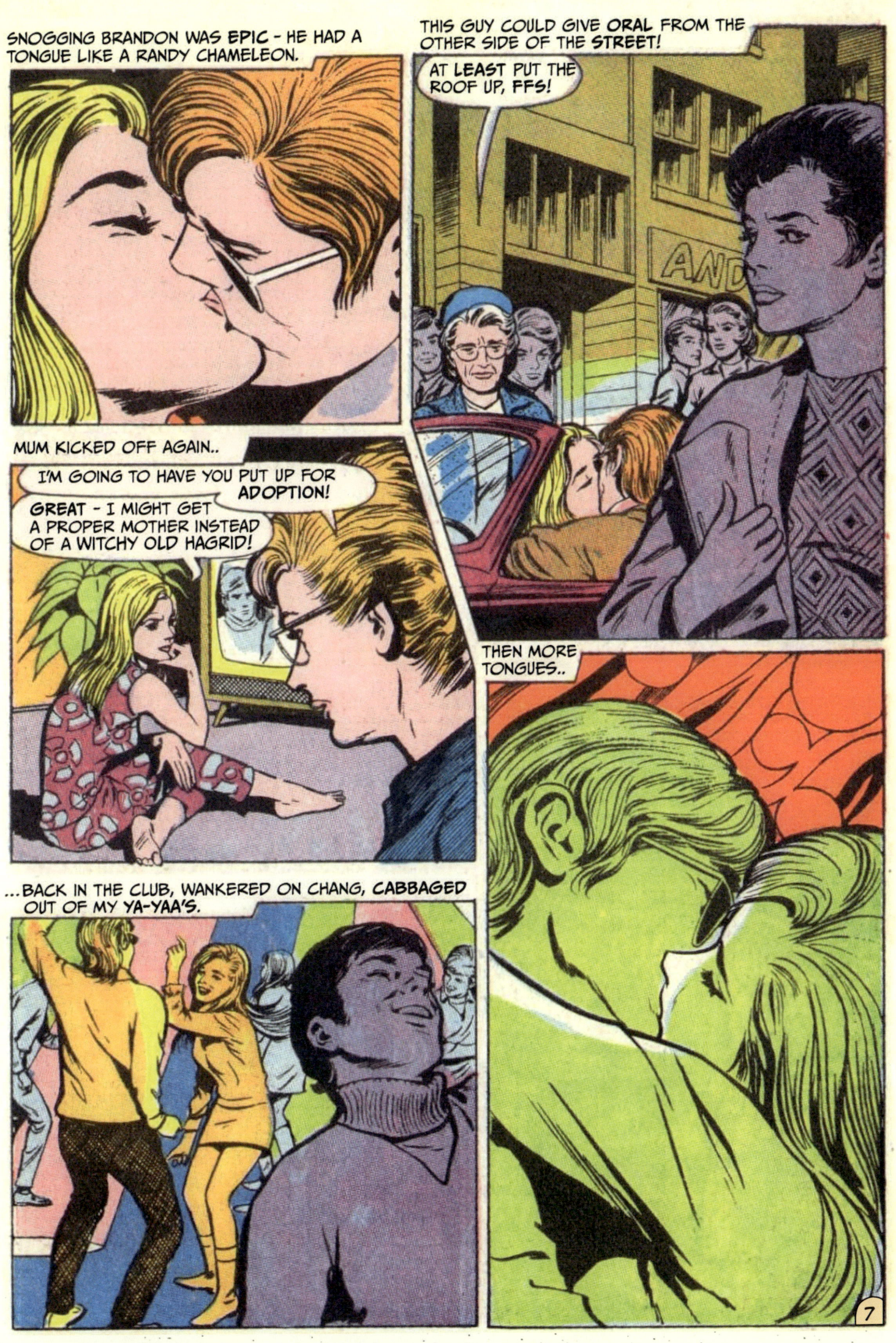

I WAS IMMEDIATELY SLUT-SHAMED BY THE RIGHT-WING PRESS AND THE REACTIONARY FORCES OF THE NEO-COLONIALIST BOURGEOIS ESTABLISHMENT.
I NEED TO CALL THE DAILY MAIL
IT'S DISGUSTING! I NEVER HAD THIS MUCH FUN!
ALL THAT FILTH IS MAKING HER YELLOW!
I JUST LIVE NEXT DOOR – I SHOULDN'T EVEN BE ON THIS PAGE.
I'VE SPENT WEEKS IN THE GYM SCULPTING MY BODY AND THE ARTIST JUST DRAWS MY FUCKING HEAD!
THEN, IN THE TOXIC MASCULINITY SECTION OF THE UNI LIBRARY, I SAW THIS GUY WHO EXUDED A MAGNETIC SENSE OF UTTER ORDINARINESS.
I'VE NEVER MET ANYONE SO LACKING IN CHARISMA EXCEPT THE GUY ON THE SUBWAY WHO TELLS YOU TO MIND THE GAP.
BUT I WAS DRAWN TO HIM LIKE A MOTH TO A CHAINSAW!
HEY, YOU LOOK DEAD SQUARE, MAN, LMAO.
BUT MAYBE YOU COULD PROVE ME WRONG?

MY REALITY **FLIPPED**: EVEN THE LEAVES HAD TURNED BLUE LIKE MY SKIRT AND BOOTS

BUT I KNEW THAT MY MOTHER WOULD TRY TO SPIN MY HEARTACHE AS BEING ALL ABOUT HER...

AS I OPENED THE DOOR SHE **LOOMED** UP AT ME, CAUSING THE TEAR WHICH HAD BEEN IN MY **RIGHT** EYE TO SUDDENLY JUMP OVER TO THE **LEFT** ONE!

I REALISED THAT WE WERE ON THE LAST PAGE OF THE STORY AND WE NEEDED A QUICK EMOTIONAL **RESOLUTION**.

SO I STOPPED SEEING BRANDON FIRSTLY, BECAUSE I WAS PRESSURED TO **CONFORM** TO THE CONVENTIONS OF THE COMIC ROMANCE GENRE WHERE THE **HEROINE** HAS TO **SUFFER** IN ORDER TO CONVEY SOME **BULLSHIT** MORAL MESSAGE! BUT **MAINLY,** BECAUSE HE RAN HIS BIKE INTO A **TREE** – THE FUCKING **IDIOT!**

YOU WERE **RIGHT!** I MUST STOP HANGING OUT WITH **UNHEP ICKYS** AND **FAPPERS!**

THERE, THERE!

BUY **COMICS REBUBBLED** TO FIND OUT WHAT HAPPENS NEXT IN THIS EPIC SAGA OF **TEENAGE ANGST.** IF YOU HAVE BEEN AFFECTED BY ANY OF THE ISSUES IN THE STORY, WE CAN'T HELP YOU. BASICALLY, LIFE **SUCKS!**

Let My Amazing SuckInYaGut Method Make YOU A New Man!

LET ME START SHOWING YOU RESULTS LIKE THESE

I can talk through my ARMPIT!

"Much more fun than talking thru my ass" —C. S., W. Va.

CURSE this toupee glue!

"My hands are stuck to my wig and my wig is stuck to my head. Please send help" —F. S., N. Y.

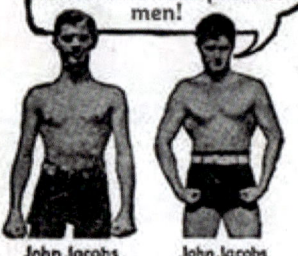

Hold your arms like this to be irresistible to women who like to fuck pretzel-men!

John Jacobs **BEFORE**   John Jacobs **AFTER**

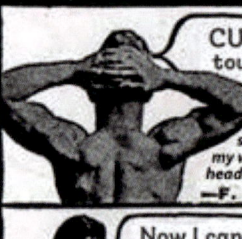

Now I can hurt any guy who makes fun of my mittens!

"Mittens are warm & very sexy" —W. G., N. J.

Refund me or I'll punch myself in the head!

"Don't make me DO it! Really. Don't. It'll hurt!" —T. K., N. Y.

CHARLES ATLAS

Awarded the title of "The World's most Perfectly Developed Man" by a panel of international voyeurs -- and all of their seeing-eye dogs. This is a recent photo of Charles Atlas showing how he looks today. Assuming today is still Wednesday. If it isn't, you're on your own. Sorry. It was Wednesday when I typed this.

Here's What Only 15 Minutes a Day Can Do For You

I DON'T care how old or young you are -- or how ashamed of your present physical condition you may be. If you can simply raise your arm and flex it, you can sign a check - made payable to 'CHARLES ATLAS *NOT A SCAM, HONEST, INC* -' and mail it to me and I will send you a fifteen page pamphlet telling you how to hold-in your tummy and point to your ears with your fists in such a way that beautiful women will be **SEXY PUTTY** in your hands... assuming you can still see your hands under all the sinew. Which you won't, because after spending just 15 minutes a day following my program in the comfort of your home you will come to resemble a giant flexed human bicep in mere WEEKS* (*assuming you also have ready access to steroids)!

What's My Secret?

Dynamic Tension!" Thats the ticket! The same way I changed my body from the scrawny, skinny-chested dipshit I was at 17, to my present super-man physique! What IS Dynamic Tension? Well, you know when you are at the gym or the pool and you notice all the guys there admiring that ONE guy with rock-hard pecs and abs you suddenly wish you were eating off? And you start to wish those other guys would look at YOU that way, even though you just agreed to move in with your girlfriend? Well, that tension you feel -- between the fact you have a girlfriend and the desire to have other men openly admiring your shapely delts -- is what I call DYNAMIC tension. And you can put it to work in helping you to extensively remodel your pathetic excuse for a body by following my revolutionary program. Every exercise is practical and, man, *so easy!* Fifteen minutes per day in your home while the girlfriend watches *Grey's Anatomy.* She won't care!

FREE BOOK
'Everlasting Health and Strength''

In it, I talk to you in straight-from-the-shoulder language, insulting your pigeon chest, laughing at your pipe-cleaner arms and berating you for not making me invent the George Foreman Grill instead. This offer CANNOT be repeated --unless you buy this publication next month. But times are hard and swimming trunks are expensive so ORDER NOWto avoid (my) disappointment.

PUDDLEMAN

THIS IS THE STORY OF HOW PROFESSOR FRANK BACONSCHLEISSER INADVERTENTLY DISCOVERED ONE OF THE GREATEST SUPERHEROES KNOWN TO THE KNOWN WORLD AND BEYOND IT.

THE PROFESSOR HAD BEEN HIRED BY HOLLYWOOD TO DEVELOP NEW FORMS OF SUPERPOWER WHICH COULD BE TURNED INTO AN ENDLESS FRANCHISE OF MIND-CRUSHING SUPERHERO MOVIES.

THESE WOULD PERPETUATE THE DOMINANCE OF THIS GENRE ON THE MINDS OF THE WORLD'S YOUTH, MAKINGTHEM PASSIVE ZOMBIES, INCAPABLE OF ANY CRITICAL THINKING.

BACONSCHLEISSER, OR B/S AS HE WAS KNOWN, WORRIED ABOUT THE MORAL IMPLICATIONS OF WHAT HE WAS DOING, BUT HE HAD FOUR KIDS, THREE EX-WIVES, TWO CATS AND A CRACK HABIT TO FUND, SO HE WAS CAUGHT BETWEEN A ROCK AND A MUCH HARDER ROCK.

PROFESSOR, WHY IS THIS COMIC SO STAINED?

NO IDEA, BOB. I'M BUSY MIXING UP SOME MORE RANDOM CHEMICALS TO SEE WHAT HAPPENS!

①

AAAGHHHH!! WHAT THE FUCK WAS THAT?

CRACK!

⑬

YOUR HAND HAS JUST **MELTED** – LIKE MY HEART DID WHEN I MET YOU!

SHUT UP WITH THE ROMANTIC SIMILES AND GET SOME **HELP**!

IS THAT A DETECTIVE?, ONE OF THE PROFESSOR'S HANDS HAS JUST **DISSOLVED**. NO HE DOESN'T HAVE BUPA BUT HE **DOES** HAVE A TESCO'S CARD. DO YOU STILL HAVE THAT OFFER ON **SPICY** DUCK **BREASTS**?

BOB, THERE'S BEEN SOME ACCIDENT WITH A LAB, AND I DON'T THINK THEY MEAN AS IN THE **DOG**!

PRWTT!

GET YOUR PANTS ON! THIS SOUNDS LIKE A **PERFECT** JOB FOR ROXY & BLAKE!

BACONSCHLEISSER'S RESEARCH IS TOP **HUSH-HUSH**. IF WE HELP HIM OUT, WE'LL BE ABLE TO RAISE OUR PROFILE AS A DETECTIVE DUO AND MAYBE EVENTUALLY HAVE OUR ADVENTURES FEATURED IN A **COMIC STRIP**!

WHAT'S THE **BANANA**, PROF?

THE **BANANA**, MY BEHATTED **FLATFEET**, IS THAT SOMEHOW I'VE CONCONCTED A **SERUM** WHICH TURNS **FLESH** INTO **LIQUID**. KIND OF WHAT THAT **JESUS** CHAP DID WITH THE **WATER** AND WINE BUT WITHOUT THE OBVIOUS SOCIAL **BENEFITS**!

14

15

MAYBE I COULD PUT THIS FREAK ACCIDENT TO GOOD USE IN THE FIGHT AGAINST EVIL, OR AS A SPECIALITY ACT IN A CIRCUS!

NOW THE SERUM MAKES YOU MORPH INTO ANY LIQUID, NOT JUST URINE! HOPE THAT'S GONNA BE A BETTER IMAGE FOR YOU....WOW MY HAND HAS COME BACK!

JAB ME UP, BABY!

I'VE GOT ALL THE ELEMENTS TO BE A SUPERHERO - A FREAK LABORATORY ACCIDENT, GIRLFRIEND WHO HARDLY TALKS, A KISS-CURL, A WELL-DRAWN JAW, AND AN UNFEASIBLY PERFECT BODY. THIS COULD BE A GREAT FRANCHISE!

YOU NEED A DISTINCTIVE COSTUME - THOSE JUSTICE LEAGUE CLOWNS LOOK SO BORING! HOW ABOUT RED CHAIN-MAIL LINGERIE, WITH A PIGSKIN JOCKSTRAP, JUDY GARLAND T-SHIRT, BOWTIE, BEIGE FLUFFY SLIPPERS, AND A FOXTAIL PROTRUDING FROM YOUR -

STOP RIGHT THERE, PROF!

SORRY, I GOT CARRIED AWAY. GOOD JOB THAT SPEECH BUBBLE WASN'T ANY BIGGER OR I'D HAVE REVEALED THE FULL RANGE OF MY FILTHY FANTASIES AND BEEN STRUCK OFF!

YOU NEED A HOMO-EROTIC NAME WHICH IS ALSO GENDER - NEUTRAL!

I'VE GOT THE PERFECT IMAGE - CRACKED FLYING GOGGLES, 26-INCH CORSETED WAIST, KINKY BOOTS, NO SHIRT, AN AMBIGUOUS CROTCH AREA AND ZERO NIPPLES! THOSE JUSTICE LEAGUE LUGNUTS BETTER STAND BACK! HERE COMES PUDDLEMAN!

AND THAT'S HOW BOB THE BOBSTER BORROWDALE BECAME PUDDLEMAN, THE GREATEST, ALL-LIQUID SUPERHERO IN THE CANON OF FIGHTERS FOR HUMAN JUSTICE!

HE'S THE BOSS, HE'S THE PIP, HE'S THE CHAMPIONSHIP HE'S THE MOST TIP TOP - PUDDLEMAN!!

TO BE CONTINUED...

16

IF HE'S A REAL PLUMBER, HOW'S HE GONNA UNBLOCK A DRAIN WITH A TOMAHAWK? WHERE'S HIS ADJUSTABLE WRENCH?

CREAK

I THINK WE'RE ACTUALLY STUCK IN A TIME WARP LIKE IN THAT MOVIE BACK TO THE FUTURE. IT'S A CLICHÉD STORY-TELLING TROPE, BUT IT'S VERY POPULAR IN THE SCI-FI GENRE.

YIP YIP

THERE'S NO POINT TRYING TO CALL THE POLICE, I DON'T THINK THE U.S. HAD 4G COVERAGE BACK IN THE 1700'S.

EEEE

BANG YIP YIP YIP

WHY HASN'T THE ARTIST DRAWN A FRAME SHOWING WHAT'S GOING ON OUT THERE? IT'S WORSE THAN A LEEDS/LIVERPOOL GRUDGE MATCH!

I GUESS HE'S WORRIED ABOUT THE NEGATIVE STEREO-TYPING OF FIRST NATION PEOPLE IN COMICS.

BLAM YIP YI

BUT HE HAS DRAWN A TRAP DOOR FOR US, WHICH IS HANDY.

GREAT! HE'S GIVING US A WAY TO ESCAPE FROM THIS STORY. IT'S OUR ONLY CHANCE OF GETTING BACK TO OUR TIME!

21

23

How to Deter a VICIOUS MONSTER at night!

As invented by Lt. Comdr 'Bobby' Dazzler Jnr, lighthouse keeper and man with a thousand yard stare.

1 You're on your way back from the pub. It's dark. You hear growling and don't know if it's a bear, a wolf or the Mindflayer from Stranger Things who's about to shove its slimy tentacles into your ears and take over your mind.

2 Shine your Vecna Flashlight directly into the monster's eyes, remember to hold it to the side and not in front of you in case the beast tries to leap at it. Always better to lost an arm than your bollocks.

This time you're lucky. It's Biscuit, next door's dog, taking a dump in the garden.

3 But next time it could be the eponymous, really gross and scary actual VECNA MONSTER from Stranger Things series 4 ---
--- in which case you'd be alerted by the soundtrack featuring 'Running up that Hill' by Kate Bush.

4 Eleven *powerful*, long-lasting batteries give you enough time to enter the Upside Down and rescue your idiot friends who shouldn't have gone down there in the first place.

DEMOGORGON TECHNOLOGY INC.
11 MKUltra Drive, Hawkins, Indiana

VECNA FLASHLIGHT

EVEREADY
TRADE-MARK
Nº 950
EXTRA LONG LIFE BATTERY
A NATIONAL CARBON PRODUCT

THE VECNA FLASHLIGHT – THE BEST WAY TO ILLUMINATE EVIL

AS THE COVID PANDEMIC SWEPT ACROSS THE GLOBE, INFECTING PEOPLE'S BODIES IN THE SAME WAY AS FOX NEWS INFECTS THEIR MINDS, PROFESSOR BACILLUS WAS MEETING TOP SCIENTISTS TO TALK CURES AND TO SMOKE COPIOUS AMOUNTS OF MEDICINAL WEED.

GENTLEMEN, WE MUST DEVELOP A VACCINE THEN SELL IT TO THE HIGHEST BIDDER, THUS CONTROLLIING THE ECONOMIES OF THE ENTIRE WORLD! WE'RE GONNA BE RICH! WOW, THIS IS GREAT BLOW MAN, I'M WHACKED OFF MY NUT!

SO, BARON VON HEISEN-SCHEISS, EMINENT SCIENTIST AND ALSO TOP GROWER OF EROTIC NOVELTY VEGETABLES, YOU WON THE GOLD MEDAL FOR THE BEST PENIS-SHAPED CARROT IN THE 2015 BAVARIAN VEGETABLE OLYMPICS, DID YOU NOT? OR DIDN'T YOU NOT? WHAT IS YOUR ANSWER, MEIN SCHATZ?

INDEED I DID OLD SAUSAGE, BUT I MUST SAY THAT I DO FIND IT OFFENSIVE TO BE PORTRAYED AS A MONOCLED GERMAN STEREOTYPE JUST TO GET SOME CHEAP LAUGHS! GERMANY IS ONE OF THE MOST PROGRESSIVE COUNTRIES IN THE WORLD WHEREAS THE UK IS HOBBLED BY NOSTALGIA FOR CORPORAL PUNISH--MENT AND THE WAR!

POINT TAKEN, SIEGFRIED, BUT I'M AFRAID THAT'S THE DEEPLY JUVENILE LEVEL OF HUMOUR YOU CAN EXPECT IN THIS COMIC - WAIT TILL THEY GET STARTED ON THE FRENCH! THEN THERE'S INNUENDO! THEY CAN'T RESIST A FART JOKE IN THE SAME WAY THAT A DOG CAN'T RESIST A LAMP POST!

TELL THEM I'D LIKE TO BE DRAWN THINNER AND MORE STYLISH, PLEASE!

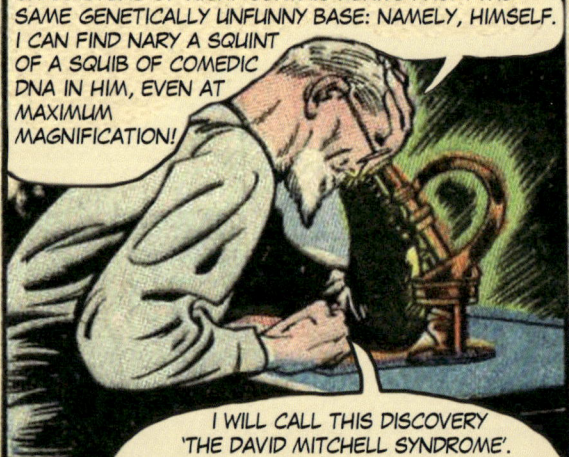

LATER, BACILLUS WAS STUDYING 'AFTER LIFE' ON HIS NEW MICROSCOPIC IPAD..

HMM I CAN OBSERVE THAT ALL THE COMEDIC CHARACTERS OF RICKY GERVAIS DERIVE FROM THE SAME GENETICALLY UNFUNNY BASE: NAMELY, HIMSELF. I CAN FIND NARY A SQUINT OF A SQUIB OF COMEDIC DNA IN HIM, EVEN AT MAXIMUM MAGNIFICATION!

I WILL CALL THIS DISCOVERY 'THE DAVID MITCHELL SYNDROME'.

THEN THE PICTURE ON BACILLUS'S WALL STARTED TO MOVE...

I HAVE IT, THE COVID VACCINE IS MINE! MINE I TELL YOU! HAHAHA! AND HAHHAA!

AAHHHH! YOU EVIL VILLAIN, THAT REALLY HURT!

I DID AN ONLINE ASSASSINATION COURSE DURING LOCKDOWN!

NOW I'LL STUFF HIS BODY PARTS INTO TESCO BAGS!

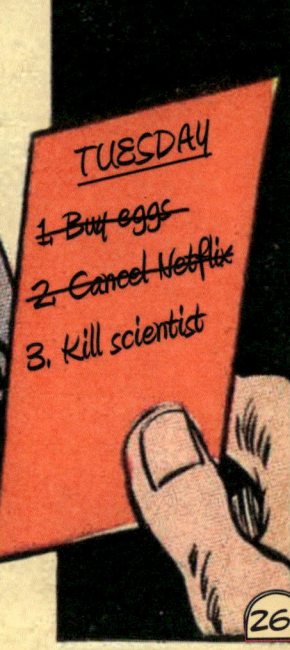

TUESDAY

1. Buy eggs
2. Cancel Netflix
3. Kill scientist

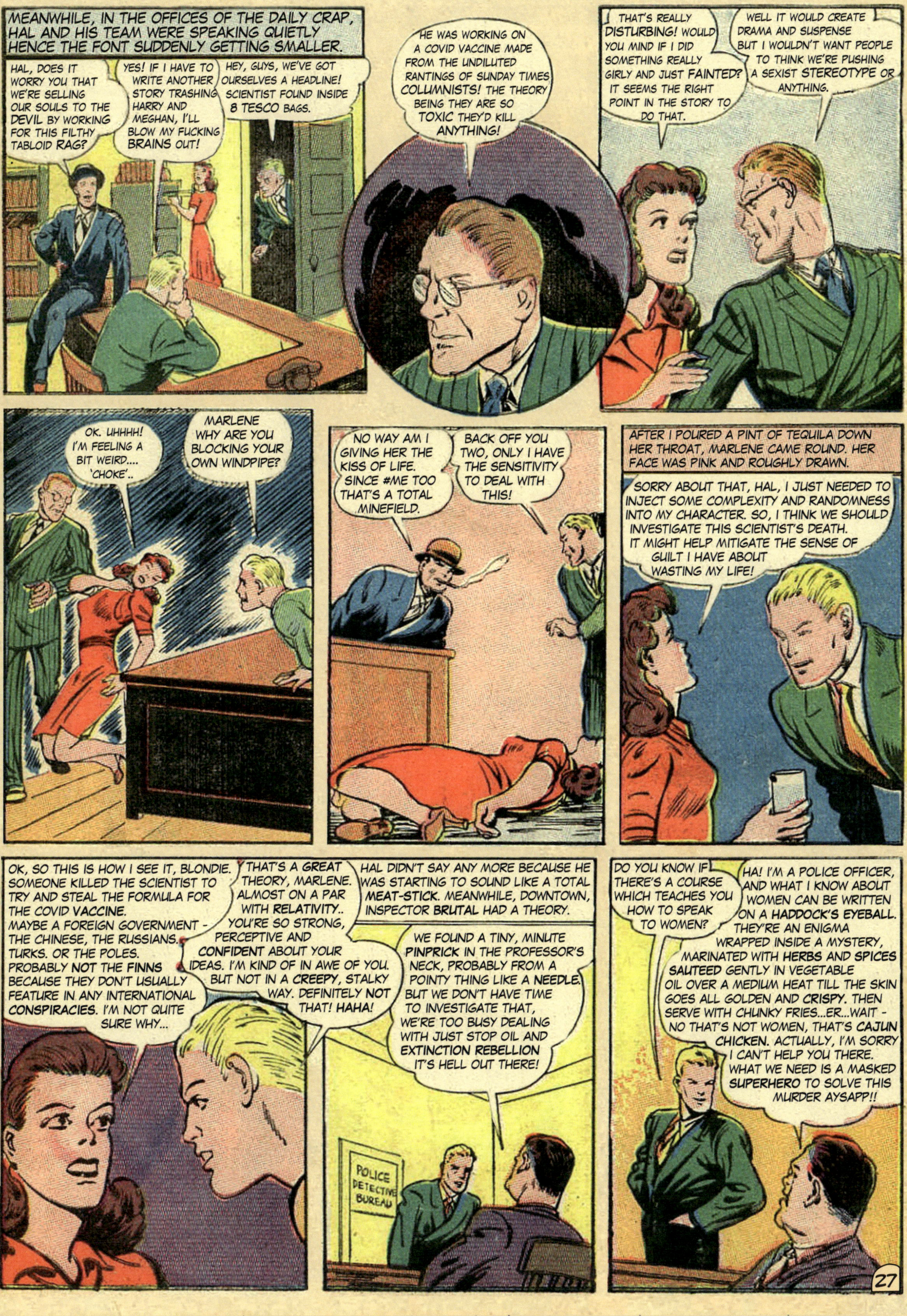

MEANWHILE, IN THE OFFICES OF THE DAILY CRAP, HAL AND HIS TEAM WERE SPEAKING QUIETLY HENCE THE FONT SUDDENLY GETTING SMALLER.

HAL, DOES IT WORRY YOU THAT WE'RE SELLING OUR SOULS TO THE DEVIL BY WORKING FOR THIS FILTHY TABLOID RAG?

YES! IF I HAVE TO WRITE ANOTHER STORY TRASHING HARRY AND MEGHAN, I'LL BLOW MY FUCKING BRAINS OUT!

HEY, GUYS, WE'VE GOT OURSELVES A HEADLINE! SCIENTIST FOUND INSIDE 8 TESCO BAGS.

HE WAS WORKING ON A COVID VACCINE MADE FROM THE UNDILUTED RANTINGS OF SUNDAY TIMES COLUMNISTS! THE THEORY BEING THEY ARE SO TOXIC THEY'D KILL ANYTHING!

THAT'S REALLY DISTURBING! WOULD YOU MIND IF I DID SOMETHING REALLY GIRLY AND JUST FAINTED? IT SEEMS THE RIGHT POINT IN THE STORY TO DO THAT.

WELL IT WOULD CREATE DRAMA AND SUSPENSE BUT I WOULDN'T WANT PEOPLE TO THINK WE'RE PUSHING A SEXIST STEREOTYPE OR ANYTHING.

OK. UHHHH! I'M FEELING A BIT WEIRD.... 'CHOKE'..

MARLENE WHY ARE YOU BLOCKING YOUR OWN WINDPIPE?

NO WAY AM I GIVING HER THE KISS OF LIFE. SINCE #ME TOO THAT'S A TOTAL MINEFIELD.

BACK OFF YOU TWO, ONLY I HAVE THE SENSITIVITY TO DEAL WITH THIS!

AFTER I POURED A PINT OF TEQUILA DOWN HER THROAT, MARLENE CAME ROUND. HER FACE WAS PINK AND ROUGHLY DRAWN.

SORRY ABOUT THAT, HAL, I JUST NEEDED TO INJECT SOME COMPLEXITY AND RANDOMNESS INTO MY CHARACTER. SO, I THINK WE SHOULD INVESTIGATE THIS SCIENTIST'S DEATH. IT MIGHT HELP MITIGATE THE SENSE OF GUILT I HAVE ABOUT WASTING MY LIFE!

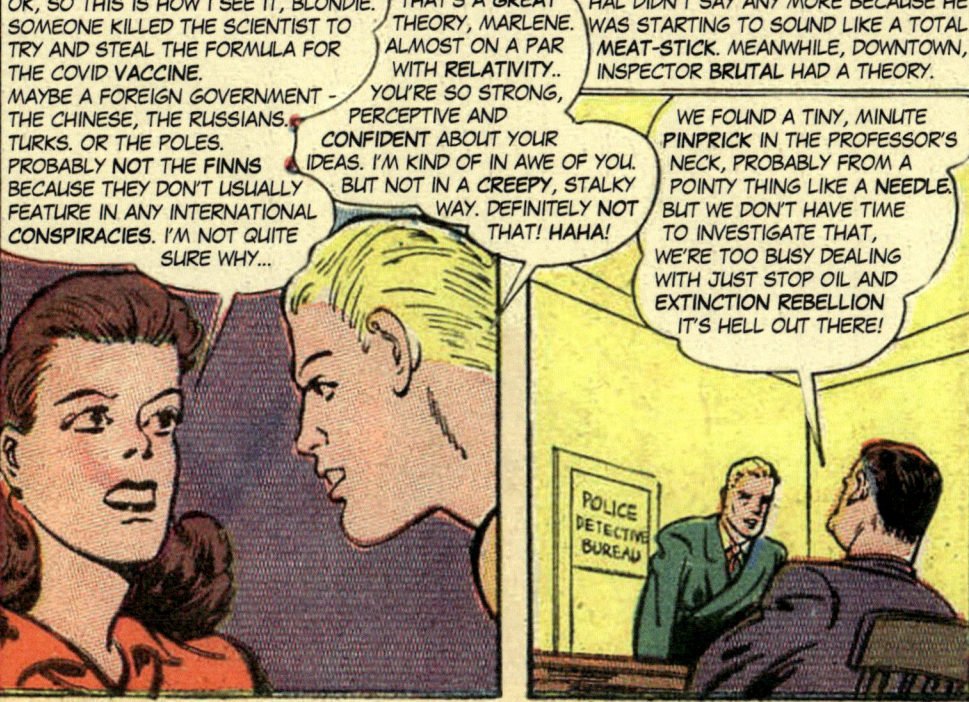

OK, SO THIS IS HOW I SEE IT, BLONDIE. SOMEONE KILLED THE SCIENTIST TO TRY AND STEAL THE FORMULA FOR THE COVID VACCINE. MAYBE A FOREIGN GOVERNMENT - THE CHINESE, THE RUSSIANS, THE TURKS. OR THE POLES. PROBABLY NOT THE FINNS BECAUSE THEY DON'T USUALLY FEATURE IN ANY INTERNATIONAL CONSPIRACIES. I'M NOT QUITE SURE WHY...

THAT'S A GREAT THEORY, MARLENE. ALMOST ON A PAR WITH RELATIVITY.. YOU'RE SO STRONG, PERCEPTIVE AND CONFIDENT ABOUT YOUR IDEAS. I'M KIND OF IN AWE OF YOU. BUT NOT IN A CREEPY, STALKY WAY. DEFINITELY NOT THAT! HAHA!

HAL DIDN'T SAY ANY MORE BECAUSE HE WAS STARTING TO SOUND LIKE A TOTAL MEAT-STICK. MEANWHILE, DOWNTOWN, INSPECTOR BRUTAL HAD A THEORY.

WE FOUND A TINY, MINUTE PINPRICK IN THE PROFESSOR'S NECK, PROBABLY FROM A POINTY THING LIKE A NEEDLE. BUT WE DON'T HAVE TIME TO INVESTIGATE THAT, WE'RE TOO BUSY DEALING WITH JUST STOP OIL AND EXTINCTION REBELLION IT'S HELL OUT THERE!

DO YOU KNOW IF THERE'S A COURSE WHICH TEACHES YOU HOW TO SPEAK TO WOMEN?

HA! I'M A POLICE OFFICER, AND WHAT I KNOW ABOUT WOMEN CAN BE WRITTEN ON A HADDOCK'S EYEBALL. THEY'RE AN ENIGMA WRAPPED INSIDE A MYSTERY, MARINATED WITH HERBS AND SPICES SAUTÉED GENTLY IN VEGETABLE OIL OVER A MEDIUM HEAT TILL THE SKIN GOES ALL GOLDEN AND CRISPY. THEN SERVE WITH CHUNKY FRIES...ER...WAIT - NO THAT'S NOT WOMEN, THAT'S CAJUN CHICKEN. ACTUALLY, I'M SORRY I CAN'T HELP YOU THERE. WHAT WE NEED IS A MASKED SUPERHERO TO SOLVE THIS MURDER AYSAPP!!

POLICE DETECTIVE BUREAU

27

NEIGHBOURS COMPLAINED AND A CRACK TEAM FROM THE MORALITY POLICE ARRIVED

WHAT'S GOING ON IN THERE?...ALL THAT BANGING AND CRASHING!

IF IT'S TWO PEOPLE BONKING, THEY NEED LESSONS! THEY'VE GOT NO RHYTHM.

WHAM! SOCK!

OPEN UP, THIS IS THE POLICE! I DID A COLLEGE MODULE IN ACHIEVING SEXUAL FULFILMENT.

ORGASM THAT, CAPTAIN COVID!

IT'S THE SEX POLICE! THE LAST THING I NEED IS SOME SWEATY COP DEMONSTRATING HOW TO PARK MY PORK GTI IN A TIGHT SPACE.

STOP FUMBLIN! HANDS UP AND AWAY FROM ANY GENITAL AREAS!

I'M CAPTAIN COVID RECAPPING THE PLOT: I'M INVESTIGATING THE DEATHS OF TWO SCIENTISTS WHO WERE RESEARCHING A COVID VACCINE THAT'S BASICALLY IT.

WELL YOUR FOREPLAY IS CRAP. AAGH!

I'VE JUST STUNNED YOU WITH MY STUN GUN BECAUSE YOU WERE ABOUT TO BREAK SOCIAL DISTANCING RULES.

CAPTAIN COVID'S CHAUFFEUR AND AMATEUR CHEF BERNARD WAITED IN HIS HUGE PHALLIC CAR

BOSS I'VE GOT CHICKEN WINGS FROM ALDI AND BULLETS FROM 'GUNS R US'

NO TIME FOR THAT, BERNIE. I'VE GOT A SYRINGE OF POISON WHICH MIGHT GIVE US A CLUE TO WHO THE MURDERER IS. BY THE WAY, I'M NOT SURE WE SHOULD BE DRIVING ROUND IN THIS MASSIVE, GAS GUZZLING PIECE OF CRAP - IT'S PROBABLY RAISING THE EARTH'S TEMPERATURE BY SEVERAL DEGREES ALL ON ITS OWN!

BERNIE WAS PISSED OFF AT THAT IDEA BECAUSE HE LOVED THE CAR. BUT HE KEPT SCHTUMM AND FLOORED IT BACK TO THE CAPTAIN'S SECRET SHAGPAD. THEN HE MARINATED THE CHICKEN WINGS AND STARTED ON THE MIX FOR A NEW SOURDOUGH LOAF.

IT DOESN'T EVEN FIT IN THE BLOODY GARAGE!

CAPTAIN COVID WAS NOT ONLY A REPORTER BUT HE HAD ALSO TRAINED FOR YEARS TO LOOK AT TINY OBJECTS THROUGH ANCIENT MICROSCOPES.

THE POISON SEEMS TO BE COMPOSED OF AN EXOTIC OIL. ALCOHOL AND ACETIC ACID. THERE ARE ALSO TRACES OF SODIUM CHLORIDE. INJECTED INTO A VEIN IT WOULD MEAN INSTANT DEATH!

THAT'S THE SALAD DRESSING YOU'RE LOOKING AT THERE, CAPTAIN!

29

WELL, SEE IF YOU GET A KICK OUT OF THIS. HAHA! SEE WHAT I DID THERE?

AAGHH! MY GUN IS NOW COMPLETELY OUT OF REACH AND USELESS TO ME!

HERE'S A PROPER LEFT HOOK TO THE JAW LIKE REAL MEN USED TO DO IN THE GOOD OLD DAYS.

FFNNGG!!

BLAT!

GET THIS HEAP MOVING BERNIE! MY GROIN'S BLEEDING LIKE A BUSTED OIL WELL AND MY SHOES ARE CLOTTING UP!

AFTER AN EMERGENCY SCROTUMECTOMY, HAL, ALIAS CAPTAIN COVID WAS BACK AT WORK.

SO THE SCOOP IS, THEY TOOK A DNA SAMPLE FROM KIM KARDASHIAN'S BUTT AND THEY FOUND MORE INTELLIGENT LIFE ON THAT PLANET THAN ON THE REST OF HER BODY.

HEY, MARLENE YOU LOOK HOT, NO SEXISM INTENDED - ANY NEWS ON THE UNMURDERED SCIENTIST BABE?

EVEN IRONY CAN BE OFFENSIVE, YOU TWAT! WELL HE'S UNDER SEVERE POLICE PROTECTION 24/7 SO IT WOULD BE TRICKY FOR ANYONE WHO TRIED TO WHACK HIM!

IT WAS TIME FOR CAPTAIN COVID TO GET INVOLVED. HE FELT IN HIS BONES THAT THE MURDERER WOULD TRY TO KILL THE REMAINING SCIENTIST AND STEAL THE VACCINE! AS HE PREPARED TO MAKE AN EMERGENCY BOWEL MOVEMENT IN HIS SHOE, HE NOTICED ANOTHER MOVEMENT UP ON THE ROOF.

ONLY A CAT OR A KILLER WOULD BE ON A ROOF THIS LATE. AND CATS DON'T WEAR TRILBYS

I'LL JUST LEAP ON THIS CONVENIENTLY-PLACED LADDER. AAAGHH! I THINK I FELT THE STITCHES POP!

THIS IS A HEALTH AND SAFETY INSPECTION - GET OFF THE BUILDING!

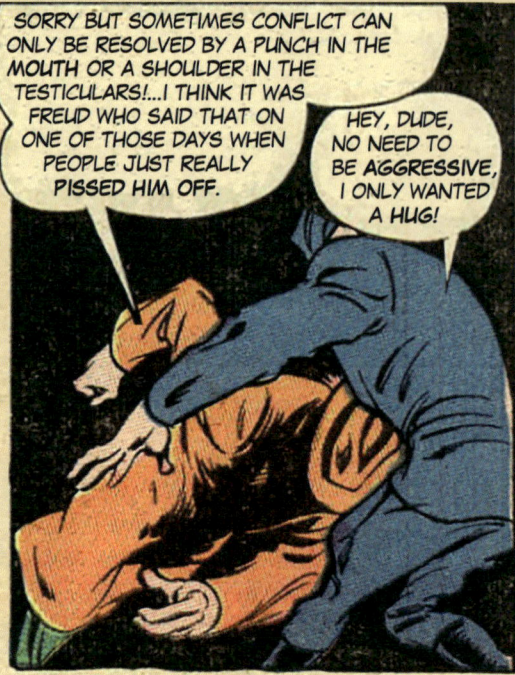

32

LEAVE ME ALONE, YOU MORONS, I'M TRYING TO SAVE THE WORLD FROM EVIL, ALTHOUGH I'M NOT SURE WHY I BOTHER.

HEY! YOU CAN'T RUN FROM YOUR FEELINGS.

LEAPING THROUGH THE AIR IS A VITAL PART OF BEING A CRIME-FIGHTER.

THE CAPTAIN'S AERIAL BALLET MOVES WERE REMINISCENT OF RUDOLPH NUREYEV IN HIS PRIME, BEFORE HE DEFECTED TO THE WEST AND BECAME CORRUPTED BY THE CAPITALIST SYSTEM.

AFTER PERFORMING A GRAND JETE FOLLOWED BY A TRIPLE PIROUETTE, THE CAPTAIN MADE A PERFECT, ONE-LEGGED SAUT DE CHAT ON THE ROOF OF HIS FAST-MOVING COCKMOBILE.

BRAVO! BUT YOU'D LOOK SO MUCH BETTER IN A LEOTARD!

SLOW DOWN A BIT, I'M NOT EFFING SUPERMAN! TAKE ME TO THE ZOO, THAT'S WHERE WE'LL FIND OUR KILLER.

THANKS FOR LENDING ME YOUR REINFORCED UNDERPANTS, BERNIE, THEY'RE PROTECTING MY TACKLE FROM BEING LACERATED AGAIN BY THIS SHARP FENCE AND ALSO HELPING THE BLOOD COAGULATE NICELY.

DON'T WORRY ABOUT GIVING THEM BACK, BOSS IT'S OK.

AH! THE MAN IN THE MASK!

WELL RECOGNISED, MATEY! SO NOW WE HAVE CURTAINS BUT STILL NO WINDOWS WHICH IS INSANE BUT IT DOES ALLOW ME TO MAKE A MORE DRAMATIC AND HIGHLY THEATRICAL ENTRANCE!

MURDER, My Sweet!

a Laura Gray: Private Investigator mystery

THANKS, MOM. SO, GUY IN A BLUE SUIT, HOW COME YOU APPEARED SUDDENLY IN OUR HALLWAY LIKE, OUT OF NOWHERE?

THE ARTIST DREW ME ON THE WRONG SIDE OF THE DOOR! I'M FROM A COMIC BOOK PUBLISHERS AND WE'D LIKE TO DO A FLY-ON-THE-WALL COMIC STRIP ABOUT YOU.

GOOD LUCK WITH YOUR FIRST CASE, LAURA, LORD KNOWS YOU NEED IT, YOUR CLOCK'S DONE TICKING, YOU STILL LIVE AT HOME WITH YOUR MAMA AND YOU DRESS LIKE A SIXTY YEAR-OLD SPINSTER!

IT WAS THE 1950'S AND EX-BRICKLAYER AND ANAESTHETIST LAURA GRAY WAS MAKING HISTORY BEING THE FIRST WOMAN OF COLOUR TO SET UP AS A PRIVATE DETECTIVE. SHE KNEW SHE WAS ENTERING A CLOSED WORLD OF WHITE, OBESE MALES WITH AN ALCOHOL PROBLEM AND AN ENLARGED PROSTATE. HOWEVER, SHE HAD JUST RECOVERED FROM A BAD BREAK-UP WITH A CIRCUS ACROBAT AND WAS KEEN TO PROVE TO HER HYPER-JUDGEMENTAL MOTHER THAT SHE WASN'T A COMPLETE DISASTER.

BASICALLY, AN ARTIST WOULD FOLLOW HER AROUND MAKING DRAWINGS AS SHE INVESTIGATED HER CASES. THEN HER STORY WOULD BE PUBLISHED AS A GRAPHIC DOCUMENTARY, INTRODUCED BY SOME CRAP COMEDIAN.

CAN YOU PICK UP MY VIAGRA PRESCRIPTION, PLEASE? THE TROUBLE IS, IF THE BAD GUYS READ THIS COMIC, THEY'LL KNOW IF YOU'RE ONTO THEM.

I KNOW, PA, BUT IT WOULD REALLY UP MY PROFILE IN THE COMIC BOOK WORLD – THOSE GEEKS ARE CRAZY ABOUT TRUE CRIME STORIES!

LAURA'S STEPFATHER

LAURA'S FIRST CASE WAS THE MURDER OF A SHOPKEEPER WHO'D BEEN CHOKED BY HAVING FIVE HUNDRED BLUE JELLY TOTS JAMMED DOWN HIS THROAT. THE GUY WAS A COUSIN OF HER NEW BF WHO SHE'D MET IN THE SOCK DEPARTMENT OF PRIMARK. HE HAD THE BIGGEST FEET IN SOUTH LONDON.

HEY, AUTRY, I'M JUST LETTING YOU KNOW WE'RE BEING DRAWN BY A COMIC BOOK ARTIST – JUST IN CASE YOU SAY ANYTHING INAPPROPRIATE.

35

IS THIS GUY GONNA WRITE DOWN EVERYTHNG I SAY? THAT'S AN REAL INVASION OF MY PRIVACY!

LOOK, BABE, I NEED ALL THE SUPPORT I CAN GET IF I'M GONNA MAKE IT IN THE DETECTIVE GAME.

FEET OFF

LAURA TOLD AUTRY SHE WAS READY TO DUMP HIS ASS IF HE DIDN'T AGREE, WHICH WOULD MEAN NO CUDDLES, NO TICKLES, NO PDA'S, BASICALLY NO NETFLIX AND CHILL EVER AGAIN. AFTER PONDERING THE IMPLICATIONS OF THIS FOR A MILLISECOND, AUTRY AGREED.

THAT SQUIRREL'S BEEN WATCHING US ALL THE TIME.

ASSUME IT'S THE ARTIST - WE CAN'T BE TOO CAREFUL!

SO TELL ME MORE ABOUT YOU - DO YOU HAVE A PERSONALITY DISORDER THAT MANIFESTS ITSELF IN SUDDEN OUTBURSTS OF - OH NO, THAT'S ME!

LET'S PUT ANY FINE ROMANCE ON HOLD UNTIL I FIND OUT WHO KILLED YOUR COUSIN BIPPY BIP.

YES, COMRADES, IT IS WEIRD FOR LAURA TO BE INVESTIGA-TING HER NEW BF'S COUSIN'S MURDER. BUT THERE ARE A LOT OF WEIRD THINGS IN THE WORLD: THE LIFE-CYCLE OF A TROUT, FURBALLS, KEITH LEMON - AND THE IDEA THAT ANYONE ACTUALLY READS THE DAILY MAIL. LAURA, WHILE SEARCHING FOR A KILLER, WAS ALSO LOOKING FOR A RELATIONSHIP WITH AT LEAST A SMUDGE OF MEANING OR SINCERITY.

BIP LOVED WEIGHING SWEETS OUT - SPECIALLY PICK 'N MIX. HE WAS A GENTLE, CARING DIABETIC. WHO'D WHACK HIM?

DID HE HAVE ANY ENEMIES IN THE CONFECT-IONERY WORLD?

Buy Comics Rebubbled

WELL, HAVE YOU HEARD OF THE KILBURN CANDY WAR? IT WAS A VICIOUS TURF BATTLE WITH ARMED GANGS FIGHTING FOR CONTROL OF THE LOOSE SWEETS MARKET - GUMMI BEARS, DOLLY MIXTURES, ALLSORTS, AND THOSE WEIRD RED AND GREEN SNAKES. LIVES TRASHED JUST FOR A HIT OF SUCROSE.

TRAGIC. IT'S A PODCAST NOW. SO, BIP WAS APPROACHED BY THE SHERBERT GANG WHO THREATENED TO MELT ALL HIS CHOCOLATE PRODUCTS WITH A HAIRDRYER UNLESS HE PAID THEM 200 QUID A WEEK IN DIME BARS, THE CREEPS.

I NEED TO TRACK DOWN THAT GANG!

LAURA KNEW THAT HER EVERY MOVE WAS BEING DOCUMENTED AND IF THE MURDERER WERE TO READ THIS COMIC, HER INVESTIG-ATION WOULD BE COMPRO-MISED. SO SHE PASSED THE TIME WITH AUTRY IN JUST GENERAL CHIRPSING CHAT...

SO, IF YOU WANNA BE MY BF, I NEED TO KNOW WHERE YOU STAND ON THE FEMALE ORGASM.

I'VE HEARD OF IT, A COUPLA MY BUDDIES HAVE SEEN ITS FOOT-PRINTS IN THE SNOW. BUT FOR ME, THE JURY'S OUT.

36

LAURA SKIPPED TRICKY TALK OF RELATIONSHIPS AND STUCK TO LESS CONTROVERSIAL TOPICS LIKE MURDER. AUTRY WAS TRYING TO BE HELPFUL BUT HIS EAGERNESS TO PLEASE, HIS OVER-HELPFUL DEMEANOUR AND DEFERENTIAL ATTITUDE WAS BECOMING A REAL PAIN IN THE STORYLINE.

BIPPY GOT A BUZZ-CUT UP THERE THE DAY HE DIED MAYBE THAT'S A LEAD?

AUTRY, THIS IS MY CASE SO WOULD YOU MIND JUST BUTTING THE HELL OUT?

I'M JUST TRYNG TO MAKE CONVERSATION - I'VE GOT A BUNCH OF SPEECH BUBBLES TO FILL UP - I'D BETTER SAY SOMETHING, OTHERWISE WHAT'S THE POINT OF BEING HERE?

TBH I'VE BEEN TRYING TO FIGURE THAT OUT!

NOT WANTING TO START OFF A DOMESTIC, LAURA DECIDED IT WOULD BE LESS HASSLE TO JUST LET HIM FLOAT ALONG BEHIND LIKE A FISHING NET SNAGGED ON THE PROPELLOR OF A HERRING TRAWLER IN THE DEEP ATLANTIC. HE SLOWED HER DOWN A BIT BUT SHE COULDN'T BE ARSED TO DIVE IN AND CUT HERSELF FREE.

SO KAYLA, WHEN YOU WERE CUTTING BIPPY'S HAIR, DID YOU NOTICE ANYTHING UNUSUAL, LIKE SOMEONE LOITERING AROUND WITH A LOOK OF MURDER IN HIS EYES?

THERE WAS A GUY SLICING UP AN AUBERGINE WITH A BIG CUT-THROAT RAZOR BUT HE'S ALWAYS HERE ON A THURSDAY.

WELL IF YOU THINK OF ANYTHING, HERE'S MY NUMBER, JUST CALL ME, MAYBE.

I CAN SENSE THAT YOU'RE SEXUALLY CONFLICTED AND AUTRY DOESN'T DUNK YOUR BISCUIT. I'M A HAIRDRESSER, I NOTICE THIS SHIT!

I'D SAY YOU BECOMING A DETECTIVE IS A METAPHOR FOR TRYING TO INVESTIGATE YOUR SEXUALITY!

TRUE, BUT THIS IS 1949 AND NON-BINARY ISN'T A THING YET.

KAYLA HAD HIT THE SPANNER ON THE NUT. I HAD TO TAKE CONTROL - WRITE MY OWN NARRATION AND DITCH THE STEROTYPE OF THE CIS-GENDERED WOMAN WHO NEEDS A MAN TO HELP HER DISCOVER WHO MURDERED HIS BROTHER. WE WERE AT THE DAWN OF A NEW DECADE - THE 1950'S: THIS WAS THE ERA WHEN, AT LAST, WOMEN WERE GOING TO BE RESPECTED AS EQUALS. OR MAYBE NOT.

SHAME YOU'RE PULLING THE CHAIN ON US, LAURA. I'M DEVASTATED AND MY SELF-CONFIDENCE IS SHOT TO FUCKRY!

YOU'RE A CUTE GUY SOMEONE'S DEF. GONNA BANG YOU WHEN THEY'RE DRUNK!

TO BE CONTINUED...

37

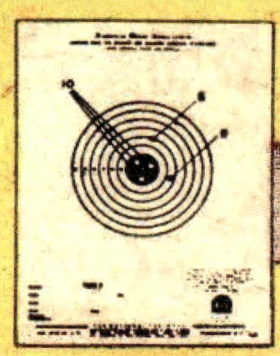

HUGO HAD ALL THE TRAPPINGS OF SUCCESS – A PUBLIC SCHOOL EDUCATION, FLASHY **CAR**, FLOPPY **HAIR**, CRAVAT, AN ADDICTION TO **PORNOGRAPHY** – BUT IT TOOK ME A FEW DATES AND A COUPLE OF DEEPLY **UNSATISFYNG** SEXUAL ENCOUNTERS BEFORE I REALISED JUST HOW **FUCKED UP** HE WAS.

Fast Cars, Handbags & Railings!

BUT DARLING – SURELY YOU **AGREE** THAT PIERS IS THE **GREATEST LIVING** ENGLISHMAN SINCE **CHURCHILL?**

OH, HUGO, HAVE SOME **SELF-RESPECT.** FIND A BETTER ROLE MODEL, LIKE **HITLER** OR **GONZO** FROM THE **MUPPETS!**

WE WOULD LIKE TO MAKE IT CLEAR THAT THE 'PIERS' IN THIS STORY REFERS NOT TO THE POPULIST CELEBRITY AND ASTUTE POLITICAL COMMENTATOR WHOSE NUANCED AND BALANCED VIEWS ARE A SHINING EXAMPLE OF THE BEST IN GRECO-ROMAN CIVILISATION.

WE ARE INSTEAD REFERENCING THE INTREPID EXPLORER MIKE, 'PIERS', MORGAN WHO HAS MADE IT HIS LIFE'S WORK TO VISIT EVERY PIER IN THE WORLD. THIS INCLUDES THE XIATAP YUARFAIS PIER IN PARAGUAY WHICH, AT 23,000 FEET, IS THE HIGHEST PIER IN THE AMERICAS. IT WAS BUILT WITH INCREDIBLE FORESIGHT IN 1643 IN ANTICIPATION OF THE RISE IN THE OCEANS DUE TO GLOBAL WARNING.

BY THE END OF 2250 IT WILL BE AT SEA LEVEL AND THE ONLY INHABITABLE STRUCTURE ON THE PLANET.

HUGO WAS A BIT OF A **KNOB**. COMING IN WITH A **CRAP** JOKE, THEN **STRAIGHT TO FIRST BASE**

HEY, THERE, SNUGGLEBUNS, I'VE CALLED THE POLICE!

THEY'RE COMING TO **ARREST** YOU - FOR STEALING MY HEART! HAHA! JUST KIDDING!!

BUT ONE DAY HE TURNED **WEIRD**..

I THINK THAT ANYONE WHO'S **WOKE** SHOULD BE TAKEN OUT, PUT UP AGAINST A **WALL** AND **SHOT!**

OH, REALLY? UMM..DON'T YOU THINK THAT'S JUST A LITTLE BIT, KIND OF - **EXTREME?**

NO WAY, BABE! LIKE THE **DAILY MAIL** SAYS, WOKERS ARE JUST LEFTIST **SCUM** WHO **THREATEN** OUR BELOVED **DEMOCRACY!**

YOU QUOTE THAT SCABBY RAG AS IF IT WERE THE BIBLE!

DAILY MAIL! THOSE TWO WORDS **REEKED** OF PREJUDICE AND COLONIALIST **NOSTALGIA**.

WE NEED YOU AND ME TIME - FORGET THE WOKERS!

I CAN'T FORGET THEM. THEY MAKE ME PUKE BIGTIME!

I'M FEELING **FRUITY** - LET'S GO TO BED - AND YOU CAN READ ME THE MOLLY **BLOOM** SOLILOQUY FROM **ULYSSES!**

40

THEN HE'D ORDER ANOTHER EMPTY PLATE BEFORE WHINGEING OFF ON ANOTHER RANT.

GUARDIAN READERS SHOULD BE FORCE-FED THE EDITORIAL PAGES TILL THEY CHOKE TO DEATH ON THEIR LIES.

BUT WHY? WHAT HAVE THEY DONE TO DESERVE THAT?

THEY'RE DESTROYING SOCIETY WITH THEIR CRYPTO-COMMUNIST, LGBTQYMCA, NEO-VEGAN IDEAS.

YOU SHOULD APPLY FOR A JOB ON GB NEWS - YOU'D BE IN GREAT COMPANY

HE FARTED ON ABOUT HOW CIVILISATION WAS BEING DESTROYED BY FAUX-LIBERAL SNOWFLAKES LIKE THE GUY SITTING AT THE NEXT TABLE - WHO WAS ACTUALLY QUITE CUTE!

WTF? HOW DO YOU KNOW THAT GUY'S A SNOWFLAKE?

BECAUSE HE'S PRETENDING TO RESPECT YOU AS A WOMAN, BUT HE'S STARING AT YOU WITH LUST IN HIS EYES WHEN I CAN SEE HE REALLY WANTS TO COLONISE YOU!

HUGO, SHUT UP! YOU'RE FOAMING AT THE MOUTH!

YOU'RE TALKING BOLLOCKS! YOU'VE HAD TOO MUCH OF THAT CHEAP ROSÉ YOU ORDERED, THINKING I DIDN'T KNOW ANYTHING ABOUT WINE.

42

ANYWAY, HE SPEWED ON LIKE LINDA BLAIR IN THE *EXORCIST*, THEN HE **ATTACKED** THE GUY ON THE NEXT TABLE.

THAT WAS SO **EMBARRASSING**, HUGO - WATERBOARDING THAT POOR GUY INTO HIS CHICKEN **CONSOMME**. LUCKY HE WAS A WORLD CHAMPION FREE DIVER OR YOU'D HAVE **DROWNED** HIM!

THOSE **FUCKING WOKERS** - THE **HYPOCRITES**. THEY GOT ME THROWN OFF X-FORMERLY-KNOWN AS-TWITTER LAST MONTH, CAN YOU **BELIEVE** IT? THEY'RE DENYING MY RIGHT TO FREE **SPEECH**,

THAT'S BECAUSE YOU CALLED FOR **WIFE-BEATING** TO BE INTRODUCED AS AN OLYMPIC EVENT!

I KNOW I'M **SHALLOW** AND I GO FOR **CISGENDERED** GUYS WITH FAST CARS, BUT YOU'RE SUCH A **DICK**, EVEN I'M HAVING SECOND THOUGHTS ABOUT HAVING **SEX** WITH YOU!

I DON'T KNOW WHAT'S GOING **ON** - MY HEAD IS FILLING UP WITH ALL THESE IDEAS AND THEY'RE MAKING ME SO **ANGRY**.

YOU CAN'T SEEM TO THINK FOR YOURSELF. WHY NOT GET ANGRY ABOUT GLOBAL **WARMING**? DO YOU REALISE THAT IN SIXTY YEARS, LIFE ON THIS PLANET MIGHT END?

AS USUAL, IF THERE WAS A STICK LYING AROUND, HUGO WAS **SURE** TO GET THE **WRONG END** OF IT.

SO IF I START CARING ABOUT ORANGE-UTANGS AND **DOLPHINS** GOING EXTINCT, WILL YOU BE LIKE, OK WITH **SHAGGING** ME?

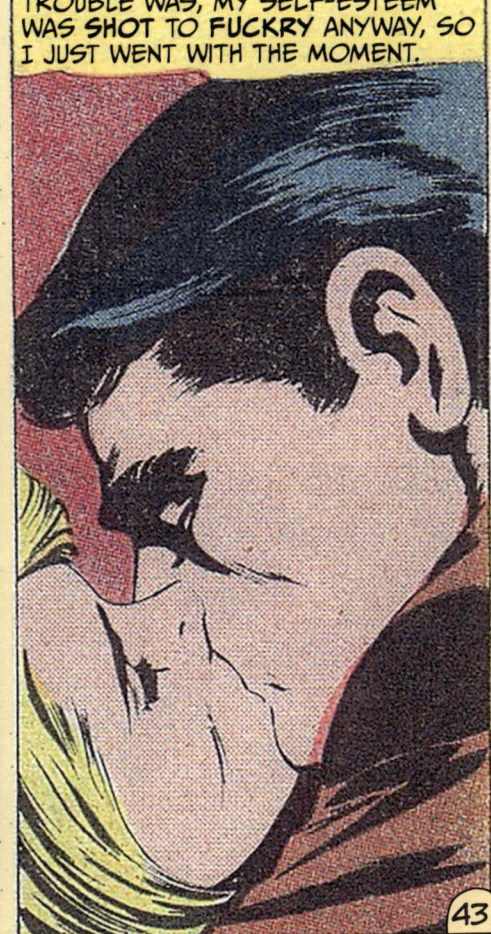

TROUBLE WAS, MY SELF-ESTEEM WAS SHOT TO **FUCKRY** ANYWAY, SO I JUST WENT WITH THE MOMENT.

43

I TRIED TO GIVE HIM A SENSE OF SOCIAL HISTORY BUT HE WAS SO **DENSE**.

12 YEARS A SLAVE? WOW, I NEVER REALISED SLAVERY WENT ON FOR 12 **YEARS**. WHAT A **DRAG**.

LAST FULL SHOW 8:40

NOW SHOWING

HE SAT THERE WITH A FACE LIKE A RAINY **MONDAY** AND A **SLAPPED ASS**, COMPLETELY **UNMOVED**...

I KNEW THIS WAS A **MISTAKE**. HE'D BE MORE COMFORTABLE WATCHING SHREK 3.

I TOOK HIS HAND OFF MY KNEE FOR THE HUNDREDTH TIME, THEN HE WENT INTO A **SULK**.

WHAT MAKES ME STILL **BELIEVE** I CAN TURN HIM INTO A **DECENT** HUMAN BEING? HE'S A TOTAL **PLANK**!

I WAS **WARY** OF TAKING HUGO INTO A DARK ROOM.

LET'S SIT IN THE MIDDLE HERE, INSTEAD OF AT THE BACK. THEN IF YOU FEEL YOURSELF GETTING A BIT **FRUITY**, YOU'LL HAVE TO SIT ON YOUR **HANDS**.

I TRIED TO DISCUSS THE IMPLICATIONS OF THE MOVIE.

WHY DIDN'T THE SLAVES SET UP **FREE** SCHOOLS AND **EDUCATE** THEMSELVES?

UH..BECAUSE THEY WERE...SLAVES?

44

BUT SURELY SLAVES COULD HAVE RAISED INITIAL **CAPITAL** ON THE **MARKETS** TO FUND A **STARTUP?** OR MAYBE EVEN **BORROWED** SOME MONEY FROM THEIR PARENTS?

HUGO, I ALWAYS KNEW YOU WERE **SUPERFICIAL**, BUT I DIDN'T REALISE YOU'RE SUPERFICIALITY WENT ALL THE WAY **THROUGH** YOU!

THAT'S A **GOOD** THING, RIGHT?

YOU'RE JUST LIKE JEREMY CLARKSON – A **COCK** ON WHEELS!

I TOLD HIM I'D ONLY BEEN SEEING HIM TO AVOID WATCHING **STRICTLY** ON SATURDAYS.

WAIT, BABE, LET'S TALK.

THERE'S **NOTHING** TO TALK ABOUT. I CAN'T DATE SOMEONE WHO THINKS THAT **BLM** IS A LUXURY GERMAN **SPORTS** CAR!

SUDDENLY HE WENT ALL **SENSITIVE** AND TRIED TO SOUND REASONABLE

OK, WE DON'T AGREE ON **EVERYTHING** – OR ANYTHING, BUT I CAN LEARN!

TOO LATE – YOU'VE BEEN **BRAINWASHED** BY THE ANTI-WOKERS. THEY'VE **INFECTED** YOUR MIND LIKE THE **POX!**

45

HE LOOKED AT ME LIKE A DUMB DOG TRYING TO SOLVE THE 'TIMES' CRYPTIC CROSSWORD.

THE POOR SOD - HE REALLY ACTUALLY DOESN'T GET IT .....

SO, LIKE A DOG, I DECIDED TO PUT HIM DOWN- HUMANELY.

HUGO, I'D JUST LIKE TO ASK, IN THE NICEST POSSIBLE WAY, IF YOU'D BE A REAL ANGEL FOR ME AND BASICALLY JUST FUCK OFF!

FOR A SECOND I WASN'T SURE I'D DONE THE RIGHT THING. BUT BY THE SECOND SECOND I WAS DEFINITELY SURE I HAD.

NOW I CAN FOCUS ON MYSELF AND FIND A DECENT NIGHTIE THAT FITS.

I FELT CLEANSED, DISINFECTED AND FREE!

LIKE FINALLY GETTING RID OF THE SMELL OF CURDLED LATTÉ FROM YOUR CAR.

AS I WAS ABOUT TO GO OUT TO CELEBRATE LIFE SANS DICKHEAD...

I LOVE A SKIRT THAT MATCHES MY HAIR.

SUDDENLY THERE HE WAS AGAIN - APPEARING AT THE DOOR LIKE A LOST FART...

PLEASE DON'T THROW ME OUT. I'VE SUDDENLY REALISED WHAT A MORON I'VE BEEN.

I DON'T WANT TO HEAR IT. I'VE MOVED ON!

46

I TOLD YOU TO NEVER AGAIN **POLLUTE** MY FLAT WITH YOUR CHEAP, **TOXIC** OPINIONS!

I WAS IN **LOVE** WITH FAR-RIGHT IDEOLOGY, NOW I KNOW IT'S ALL **SHIT!**

YOU WERE QUOTING JOE **ROGAN** LIKE HE WAS SOME KIND OF PIMPED-UP **DALAI LAMA!** SO HOW COME YOU'VE CHANGED?

WELL, THE REASON I FELT DRAWN TOWARDS THE MACHO, ALT-RIGHT WAS BECAUSE, LIKE ALL OF THEM, I'M INSECURE WITH A SMALL **PENIS!**

HUGO SPELT OUT 'PLEASE FORGIVE ME' IN ALPHABETTI SPAGHETTI AND SERVED IT UP FOR DINNER.

NOW I SEE THROUGH THOSE HACKS LIKE **DIMWHITT,** CONYO, TINYCOCK, PIZZLE AND I'M **NOT** BEING REBUBBLED, THIS IS **ME** TALKING!

BELIEVE ME, SNUGGLEBUNS! I'VE FINALLY **ESCAPED** THE CLUTCHES OF THOSE FASCIST, NEO-COLONIALIST **STATUE-HUGGERS.** I'M PROPER ANTI, ANTI-WOKE!

NICE WORDS, BUT HOW DO I KNOW YOU'RE NOT SAYING WHAT I WANT TO HEAR JUST TO GET INTO MY JIMJAMS?

BECAUSE I'M A FEMINIST NOW, AND I'VE STARTED LISTENING TO **WOMAN'S** HOUR!

AS HE PRESSED HIS PREJUDICES AGAINST ME, I KNEW I HAD TO RID MYSELF OF THIS DAMAGED MAN-CHILD.

HMM.. I MUST PICK UP A **CORNICHON** FROM WAITROSE!

HOW TO HYPNOTIZE IN 25 EASY LESSONS!

Exert your hypnotic power over others without them realising! Amaze your friends! Punish your enemies! Astound and astonish people you don't even know!

Yes, it's unbelievable! This book will unlock the ancient secrets of ancient civilisations that are really, really old.

Like the ancient Egyptians, the old Galtiberians of Gallalacia and the Cornishons of Cornwall.

Priests, mystics and shamans study and meditate for years to master these techniques. I can give them to you in the time it takes to read my book.

HYPNOTIZE MUGGERS
Make them give you their phone instead of stealing yours

HYPNOTIZE A POLICEMAN
When stopped for speeding, make him think he stopped you to compliment you on your driving skills.

HYPNOTIZE YOUR PET
Stop it doing its business on the carpet and auto-suggest that it climbs through the fence and shits on the neighbor's patio instead.

HYPNOTIZE YOUR MOM
So she forgets that time when she walked into your bedroom to find you fapping into an old sock.

Some bloke

25 MIRACLE LESSONS

I CAN HELP PUT THE 'ME' INTO MESMERIZE!

MAGNETIC INFLUENCE

- Bend iron filings to your will.

THE POWER OF SUGGESTION

- You WILL buy my book.

SEDUCE MEMBERS OF THE OPPOSITE SEX

-or just stop them biting their nails. Or both! At the same time!

CURE ALL BAD HABITS

- except for relentless over-promising.

READ MINDS

-- so much cheaper than audiobooks!

SPECIAL OFFER FOR READERS OF *COMICS REBUBBLED*

Try out for 30 days without obligation then if you aren't satisfied, return the book and we will refund your money. OR, if you are clever, Keep the book and hypnotise us to believe that you have returned it. Then you'll get the money back as well!!

Palme-Jones Publishers, Dot. 325, 235 Market St., Newark, N.J.

HYPNOTIZE GIRLS
Make them think you are a GOD with a tool like the handle of a coal miner's shovel and the sexual prowess of a wild Californian Mustang.
(NOTE: Above technique may not work as most girls are currently much too smart to fall for that shit.)

HYPNOTIZE GUYS
Stop their leering and perving and watch them turn into human beings who respect you as an equal.
And if that doesn't work, then:

HYPNOTIZE YOURSELF
To convince yourself that it has.

And for those who can't be arsed to read my book, we offer --

HYPNO-COIN
NEW - POCKET SIZE INVENTION HELPS HYPNOTIZE IN MINUTES

SO easy to use.
Even easier than writing a story for the Mail Online.

Hold the HYPNO-COIN in front of the hypnotee and vibrate the plastic lens, producing a hypnotic pattern similar to the rubbish special effects of a 1960's episode of Doctor Who, a motion more fascinating than even a prima ballerina dancing Swan Lake in a pair of Classic brown suede Uggs. (£131.99 From John Lewis)

Once entranced, your friends can be exploited for entertainment value as you make them run round a shopping mall trouserless, shouting: 'Yes I do believe in trickle-down economics'

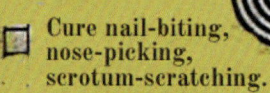

CHECK HERE HYPNOTIC POWERS YOU WANT!

☐ Appear smarter than you are

☐ Cure nail-biting, nose-picking, scrotum-scratching.

☐ Cure your fear of clowns (even Jacob Rees-Mogg)

ALL OF US HAVE ASKED IT: *WHERE DO I COME FROM? WHAT IS MY PURPOSE? WHY DOES NETFLIX AUTOPLAY THE NEXT EPISODE BEFORE THE CURRENT ONE'S EVEN FINISHED?* TWO-THIRDS OF THESE ARE THE *SAME* QUESTIONS MAN'S BEEN ASKING SINCE HE CRAWLED FROM THE PRIMEVAL BOG AND WONDERED 'WHAT THE HELL WAS I EVEN *THINKING* JUMPING INTO A PRIMEVAL BOG?'. COME WITH US NOW AS WE SQUINT THROUGH THE MILLENNIA TO *ANSWER* THOSE QUESTIONS AND GET BACK, GET BACK, GET *BACK* TO WHERE WE ONCE BELONGED...

...WHEN DICKHEADS RULED THE EARTH*

* as they still do.

EVERY SEASON, TEAM-MATES *FRED* AND *BARNEY* WOULD HELP PREPARE THEIR TEAM'S KIT FOR THE LOCAL *DERBY*..!

BARN, DOES IT GET ANY BETTER THAN THIS? TWO BRO'S SHARPENING THEIR *POINTY-STICKS* TOGETHER! TRULY THIS IS THE GOLDEN AGE OF TECHNOLOGY!

GOLDEN AGE? DUDE, WE'RE WEARING *FUR NAPPIES*, WE'RE HALF-NAKED, ONLY 5 PEOPLE HAVE 'LIKED' MY PAINTINGS ON *INSTACAVE* AND THE AVERAGE LIFE EXPECTANCY IS *'NEXT TUESDAY'*! BUT AT LEAST WE GET TO KICK THE ASSES OF THE PONCE-HEAD TRIBE TOMORROW..!

ON THE OTHER SIDE OF *UG VALLEY*, TWO OF THE PONCE-HEAD TRIBE WERE ALSO REFLECTING ON TOMORROW'S BIG GAME...

QUINTON, I *HATE* MY HAIR. IT'S *PREHISTORIC*! LEVEL WITH ME, COULD I PULL OFF A *MAN-BUN*?

IT WOULD HIDE YOUR *SPLIT-ENDS*, BUT TEAM MORALE IS LOW. IF WE DON'T WIN TOMORROW'S *POINTYSTICK* MATCH WE'LL BE RELEGATED TO THE CRO-MAGNON ISTHMIAN LEAGUE!

THE *INCEL* TRIBE'S ON A ROLL. WORD IS THE CAPTAIN'S *B.O* CAN KILL A MAN FROM CLEAN ACROSS THE SIX-YARD LINE.

49

DON'T WORRY, JAMAR. I WILL ASK THE *SHAMAN* ABOUT MORALE. ASK HIM TO INVENT US A NEW WEAPON TO SMITE THE INCELS IN THE *SMITIEST* WAY POSSIBLE. NOW LET US LEAVE THIS PLACE --THAT TINY *DINOSAUR* OVER THERE IS FREAKING ME OUT....

I'M A FUCKING *IGUANA..!*

QUINTON AND JAMAR EXPLAINED THEIR FEARS TO THE PONCE-HEADS' FAMED PROPHET AND SHAMAN, *VON DÄNIKEN*

TOMORROW? SERIOUSLY?? YOU THINK I PULL THESE INVENTIONS OUT OF MY *ARSE?* I HAVE TO WANDER THE WILDERNESS ON A *VISIONQUEST...* SEEKING INSPIRATION... ENLIGHTENMENT. IT'S A WHOLE *THING.* I NEED TWO DAYS TO MAKE THE *SANDWICHES..!*

TAKE SOME BREAD AND FIND A TINY DINOSAUR ON THE WAY

THEY'RE FUCKING *IGUANAS...!*

AND SO, VON DÄNIKEN BEGAN HIS *QUEST...*

HEY, YOU THINK WE SHOULD HAVE ASKED HIM FOR MORE STUFF? LIKE MAYBE TO INVENT *WOMEN* BEFORE MATING SEASON STARTS?

AS THE GUY YOU MATED WITH LAST SEASON, I GOTTA SAY -- I'M *SO* OFFENDED!

VON DÄNIKEN WAS GRUMPY BECAUSE HE HAD A *SECRET;* ONE HE KNEW HE COULD NEVER SHARE...

IF THE TRIBE KNEW ALL OUR ADVANCES... SPEARS, FIRE, *SCRUNCHIES...* CAME NOT FROM ME BUT FROM GODS BEYOND THE SKY, THEY'D BE BUMMED!

FINALLY VON DÄNIKEN REACHED THE *CAVE OF AWE,* WHERE MANY YEARS AGO HE'D WATCHED A *CHARIOT OF THE GODS* PARALLEL PARK...

HEAR ME, CELESTIAL BEINGS - IT IS I, *VON DÄNIKEN* SEEKING WISDOM AND *CLARITY.* AND IF YOU'VE GOT A COUPLE OF SANDWICHES, I'LL TAKE THEM AS WELL...

AN ANCIENT *HUM* ECHOED FROM THE CAVE AND A BRIGHT *LIGHT* BURNED LIKE GOD'S *EYE..!*

MY TRIBE ARE SCARED OF GETTING THE *SHIT* KICKED OUT OF THEM BY THOSE NO-NECKED *REDNECKS* ACROSS THE VALLEY. AND THEY ARE FEELING A GREAT ABSENCE OF LOVE IN THEIR LIVES. *HELP* US, OH SKY-GODS!

THE *HUM* INTENSIFIED AND THEN... EMERGING FROM THE *DAZZLING BRIGHTNESS...*

WE HAVE HEARD YOUR PLEAS. WE REGRET, THE KITCHEN IS NOW CLOSED, BUT IF YOUR PEOPLE LACK LOVE, PLEASE ACCEPT THIS CUPID'S BOW AND ARROW. WHOSOEVER YOUR PEOPLE SHOOT WITH THIS ARROW WILL FALL INSTANTLY *IN LOVE* WITH THEM....!

50

SKYGODS, WE THANK YOU. IT *MIGHT* BE BETTER TO CREATE SOME HOT BABES FIRST, *THEN* A WAY TO MAKE THEM FALL FOR US, BUT YOU ARE MIGHTY IN YOUR WISDOM EVEN IF YOUR KITCHEN HOURS ARE RIDICULOUS.

THE LIGHT GLOWED *BRIGHTER* AS THE MIGHTY INTELLIGENCE PROCESSED THE SHAMAN'S WORDS AND --

THANK YOU FOR YOUR FEEDBACK - WE CONSTANTLY STRIVE TO *IMPROVE* OUR OFFERING AND WILL FORWARD YOUR COMMENTS TO THE APPROPRIATE DEPARTMENT...

ALRIGHT - I THINK THAT WENT PRETTY *WELL*...EXCEPT FOR THE SANDWICH. I'M SODDING RAVENOUS AND --- MMMMMM, THAT 'BOW' THING LOOKS *DELICIOUS*..!

BY THE TIME VON DÄNIKEN RETURNED, THE BOW HAD BECOME A LOW CALORIE SNACK AND THE TRIBE HAD TO RECONSTRUCT IT FROM MEMORY....

SORRY I ATE THE PROTOTYPE--BURP!--BUT ACCORDING TO, ER, MY *VISION*, THESE THINGS WILL CHANGE OUR LIVES!

MMMM -- *BENDY*..!

THIS IS *SHIT*. WE NEED BETTER POINTYSTICKS OR SOME FIT BIRDS, NOT A CURVY SODDING *TWIG*!

YOU ARE SO GODDAM *SNIPPY* TODAY, AKON! WHO PUT AN IGUANA UP *YOUR* ASS??

IT'S NONE OF YOUR BUSINESS *WHERE* I KEEP MY PETS!

QUINTON *RELEASED* THE ARROW AND --

THE BENDYSTICK *WORKS*! IF WE USE IT TO SHOOT LOVE-TWIGS AT THE INCELS, WE'LL MAKE THE WHOLE *TRIBE* FALL IN *LOVE* WITH US...!

THWOCK!

THE NIGHT BEFORE THE BIG GAME, CONSTRUCTION OF THE *BENDYSTICKS* CONTINUED APACE...

IF WE CAN MAKE THE INCELS LOVE US ENOUGH TO *CONCEDE* THE MATCH TO US...

...WE'LL GO THROUGH TO THE POINTYSTICKS NATIONAL FINAL AGAINST THE *GRYFFINDOR TRIBE* -- THOSE SPOOKY LITTLE FUCKERS.

51

NEXT DAY ON UG VALLEY'S POINTYSTICKS PITCH, THINGS *KICKED OFF*..!

FLANKING FOR THE *UG VALLEY UNIBROWS!* BARN, DOES IT GET ANY BETTER?

WE'VE *HAD* THIS CONVERSATION FRED - I BLOODY WELL *HOPE SO*..!

THE *PONCE-HEAD PONCERORS* HAD WON THE SHELL-TOSS AND TAKEN THEIR POSITION ON THE DEFENSIVE MOUND

THEY'RE COMING! I NEED EVERY MAN TO *GRAB* HIS BENDYSTICK!

THE SUDDEN *RAIN OF ARROWS* TOOK THE UNIBROWS *TOTALLY* BY SURPRISE..!

WTF?? MINI POINTY-STICKS! *MILLIONS* OF THEM AND--EUGGHHH, ONE'S GONE THROUGH ALVIN'S *HEAD!* IS THE REF EFFING *BLIND*??

ZIP!

ZIP!

TWANG!

THE REF WAS, IN FACT, BLIND AS A 'MINI-POINTYSTICK' HAD JUST PUNCTURED *BOTH* HIS EYEBALLS. FRED *FLED*...

ARGGHHH! MUST GET AWAY! FASTER...FASTER! *CURSE* THE WIND RESISTANCE CAUSED BY MY COPIOUS *BODY-HAIR!*

AND FRED *RAN* AS FAST AS HIS *FURRY LEGS* WOULD CARRY HIM...!

THEY'RE NOT FALLING IN *LOVE*, SHAMAN - THEY'RE JUST... *FALLING.*

GUESS IT'S HARD TO FALL IN LOVE WHEN YOU'RE *BLEEDING* TO *DEATH* WITH A HOLE IN YOUR HEAD. *SORRY*, QUINTON, THIS IS NOTHING LIKE WHAT I WAS TOL-- ER, *EXPECTING!*

AT LEAST WE WON THE GAME. *AND* WE KNOW PENETRATING SOMEONE WITH YOUR LOVE-TWIG IS ABSOLUTELY *NO* GUARANTEE THAT THEY WILL LIKE YOU.

NOT UNLESS YOU'VE SHARED SOME *CHARRED MAMMOTH* AND A COUPLE OF GLASSES OF *FIREWATER* FIRST ANYWAY...

MEANWHILE, THE INCELS HAD STARTED CONDUCTING THEIR POST-MATCH *ANALYSIS*...

LET'S GO BACK OUT THERE AND GIVE THE FLOPPY-HEADED BASTARDS A HIDING!

GO *BACK*? ER, NO THANKS BARNEY. YOU GO. I WAS PLANNING TO STAY *IN* TONIGHT AND WEAVE A *NAPKIN* FROM MY CHEST-FUR.

53

THE BOULDER *PLUNGED* DOWN THE CLIFF, *SMASHING* THROUGH THE ROOF OF THE CAVE - AND CRASHING ONTO A STRANGE *METAL VEHICLE* -- WHICH IT *SHATTERED*..!

LOOK, BARNEY - *RUBBLE*! AND--IS THAT...A CELESTIAL *CHARIOT*??

SO IT'S TRUE --GOD *WAS* AN ANCIENT ASTRONAUT!

NOT WAITING TO SEE IF THE CHARIOT HAD A *DASHBOARD-CAM*, THE INCELS LEGGED IT WITH THE EVIDENCE...

HEY GUYS - IS IT JUST ME OR IS THIS ONE *FLAMING SEXY* BOULDER? JUST GET A LOAD OF THOSE HOT *CURVES*! HUBBA-HUBBA !!!

IT'S JUST YOU, FRED...

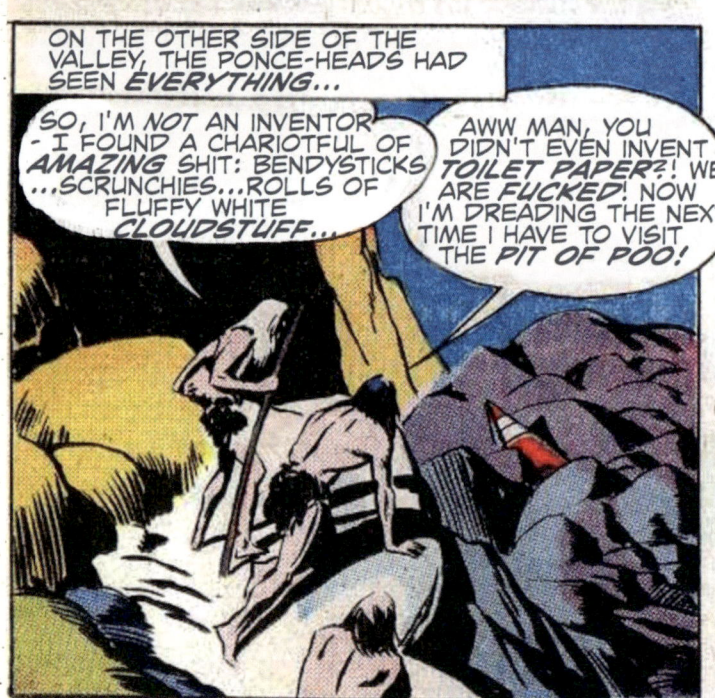

ON THE OTHER SIDE OF THE VALLEY, THE PONCE-HEADS HAD SEEN *EVERYTHING*...

SO, I'M *NOT* AN INVENTOR - I FOUND A CHARIOTFUL OF *AMAZING SHIT*: BENDYSTICKS ...SCRUNCHIES...ROLLS OF FLUFFY WHITE *CLOUDSTUFF*...

AWW MAN, YOU DIDN'T EVEN INVENT *TOILET PAPER*?! WE ARE *FUCKED*! NOW I'M DREADING THE NEXT TIME I HAVE TO VISIT THE *PIT OF POO*!

IT'S FOR THE BEST. WE RELY TOO MUCH ON STRANGE TECHNOLOGY WE DON'T UNDERSTAND AND CAN'T *CONTROL*. MAYBE IT'S TIME TO STAND ON OUR OWN *TWO FEET*..!

TELL YOURSELF THAT WHEN YOU'RE STANDING ON *YOUR* OWN TWO FEET SQUATTING OVER THE PIT OF POO AND WIPING YOUR *ARSE* WITH A *STINGING NETTLE*! DO WE EVEN KNOW WHERE THE CHARIOT *CAME* FROM?

FROM BEYOND THE STARS; A PLACE SO *SUPERIOR*, ITS PEOPLE SOMETIMES ACTUALLY DISDAIN *SANDWICHES*! WE ARE NOT WORTHY OF SUCH A SPECIES!

TOILET PAPER WILL *NEVER* BE EQUALLED, BUT MAYBE SOMEDAY WE'LL INVENT A PLASTIC WALL-HANGING FISH THAT *SINGS* OR A CANDLE IN THE SHAPE OF A *PENIS* AND WE TOO CAN TAKE OUR PLACE AMONG THE GODS!

IF THE SHAMAN OR THE PONCE-HEADS HAD *PAUSED* BEFORE HEADING BACK TO A WORLD WITHOUT *MIRACLES* OR SANITARY PRODUCTS, THEY'D HAVE SEEN A MACHINE *CLICK* ON IN THE WRECKAGE, AND HEARD THE VOICE OF A LONG-DEAD *GOD*..!

HI THIS IS ELON MUSK. I'M TOO *RICH* TO COME TO THE PHONE RIGHT NOW. PLEASE PRESS '1' IF YOU WANT TO BUY A BIG BATTERY IN THE SHAPE OF *A CAR*...

...PRESS '2' IF YOU WANT ME TO SHOOT YOU INTO *SPACE* AND PRESS '3' IF YOU WOULD LIKE ME TO *OVERPAY* FOR YOUR SOCIAL MEDIA PLATFORM THEN *TRASH* IT.

THE END!

6

THE FALL OF SCOTT GIGAWATT

HI THERE, I'M SCOTT GIGAWATT. I FLY ROUND THE UNIVERSE PROTECTING THE EARTH FROM BEING DESTROYED BY THINGS LIKE THIS MASSIVE ASTEROID WHICH I'M ABOUT TO SMASH UP. RECENTLY I ATTACKED A GIANT NUCLEAR ROBOT WHICH WAS THREATENING TO ANNIHILATE THE HUMAN RACE FOR NO PROPER REASON. HE WAS AN ARROGANT BASTARD AND HE PISSED ME OFF. THIS IS THE STORY OF WHAT HAPPENED.

OUR STORY BEGINS WITH SCOTT, HIS POWERS EXHAUSTED AND HIS LATEX SUPPORT SHORTS AFLAME, HURTLING HORRIFICALLY THROUGH SPACE AND KERRASHING COMICALLY TO EARTH. HE IS MEDIVACKED TO THE GOTHAM HOSPITAL FOR BADLY KIBOSHED SUPERHEROES. Now read on.

GOTHAM GENERAL

HEY DOC, IS THAT SCOTT GIGAWATT? WHERE'S HIS SEXY YELLOW ONESIE?

WELL, SERENA, AS HE FELL TO EARTH, HIS BODYSUIT DISINTEGRATED, SO RATHER THAN BRING HIM IN NICKY NACKY NAKED, WE DRESSED HIM IN HIS OFF-DUTY LOUNGE-LIZARD OUTFIT

EMERGE

Today's schedule
2.15pm De-claw Wolverine
3.05pm Hawkman bird-flu jab
5.00pm Iron-Man annual rust inspection
5.40 Incredible Hulk vasecto

LUCKILY HE LANDED ON A LIDL CAR PARK INSTEAD OF A CHURCH SPIRE OR WE'D BE DEALING WITH A HUMAN KEBAB!

I'LL FEED HIM SOME NITROUS OXIDE THROUGH THIS SLINKY JUST FOR A GIGGLE! A BIT OF FUN ALWAYS HELPS AN NHS HOSPITAL FEEL LESS LIKE A HELL-HOLE!

I TOLD YOU THAT FLYING AROUND THE SOLAR SYSTEM WAS STUPID AND DANGEROUS!

THAT'S CANDICE, SCOTT'S NEW GIRLFRIEND. THEY MET IN IBIZA AFTER HE'D SAVED THE PLACE FROM BEING DESTROYED BY A MUTANT ALIEN DJ HIGH ON DONKEY DUST!

BUT SCOTT SAID HE WAS GIVING UP THIS SUPERHERO NONSENSE.. I'VE PUT OUR NAMES DOWN FOR AN ALLOTMENT AND JUST BOUGHT A DARLING COCKAPOO.

HE'S JUST FALLEN A MILLION MILES THROUGH SPACE AND LANDED ON HIS COCCYX. HIS MIND'S NOT EXACTLY FOCUSED ON PLANTING VEGETABLES OR SCOOPING UP DOG POOP..

I DON'T KNOW WHY HE'S SO KEEN TO SAVE HUMANITY, WHAT WITH GLOBAL WARMING AND PANDEMICS - THE WORLD'S COMPLETELY RUBBER-DUCKED! I SAID LET'S GET A BUNGALOW ON MARS, IT'S SO CHEAP THERE AT THE MOMENT..

MY MUM WAS RIGHT. "DON'T GO NEAR SUPERHEROES", SHE TOLD ME: "YOU'LL ALWAYS COME SECOND TO A PLANE CRASH OR AN EARTHQUAKE". BUT I DIDN'T LISTEN TO HER AND I FELL IN LOVE WITH HIM, LIKE AN IDIOT!

BUT I DON'T WANT TO LOSE HIM, SO PLEASE DOSE HIM WITH EVERYTHING YOU'VE GOT: ASPIRIN, POXYMOXYDOL, KETAMINE, TARGARYEN, NOVAQUINE, FREDDIMURKYQUINE, WHATEVER..

DON'T WORRY, I'VE SEEN THIS WITH SUPERHEROES BEFORE. THEY PUSH THEMSELVES TOO FAR AND JUST BURN OUT. WE HAD BATMAN IN HERE A FEW WEEKS AGO - HE WAS HAVING MASSIVE MIGRAINES AND BLADDER PROBLEMS, I MEAN, HE WAS CRYING SO MUCH WE HAD TO PUT A SPONGE LINING INSIDE HIS MASK AS WELL AS HIS PANTS!

THE BEST THING FOR YOU IS LEAVE IT TO THE SURGEONS, GO HOME, DRINK A BOTTLE OF SAUV BLANC, DRUNK-TEXT YOUR EXES TILL ONE COMES OVER AND YOU REALISE WHY YOU DUMPED HIM BUT HAVE SEX ANYWAY, THEN FEEL LIKE CRAP. GO ON..

THAT'S GREAT ADVICE. I'D LOVE TO DO A USEFUL JOB LIKE YOURS. IT MUST BE SO REWARDING TO HELP PEOPLE OVERCOME A CRISIS IN THEIR LIVES WHILE COVERED IN SNOT AND BODILY FLUIDS.

YES, WELL THAT'S ONE WAY OF LOOKING AT IT. SO YOU TODDLE OFF AND WE'LL SLICE HIM OPEN AND TAKE A SQUINT IN THERE TO SEE WHAT'S STOPPING HIM FLYING ABOUT.

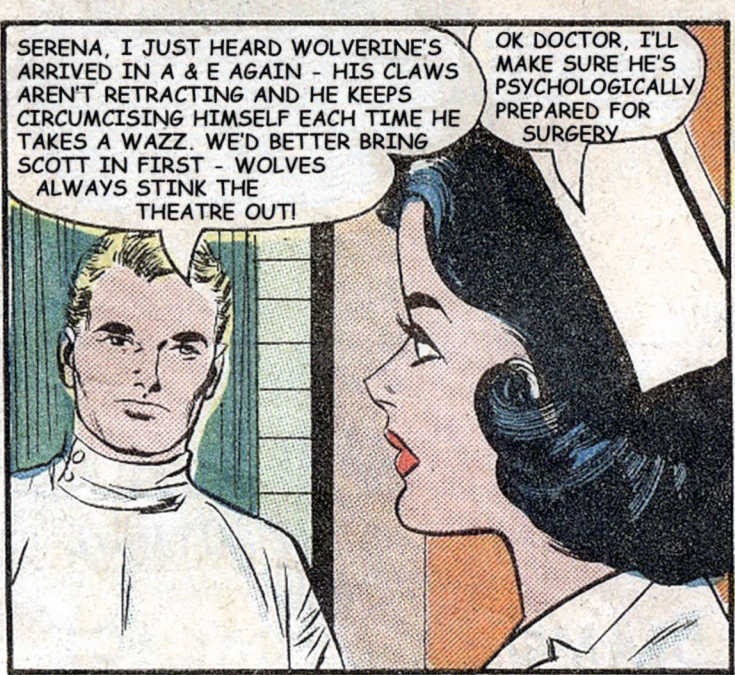

SERENA, I JUST HEARD WOLVERINE'S ARRIVED IN A & E AGAIN - HIS CLAWS AREN'T RETRACTING AND HE KEEPS CIRCUMCISING HIMSELF EACH TIME HE TAKES A WAZZ. WE'D BETTER BRING SCOTT IN FIRST - WOLVES ALWAYS STINK THE THEATRE OUT!

OK DOCTOR, I'LL MAKE SURE HE'S PSYCHOLOGICALLY PREPARED FOR SURGERY

HI SCOTT, YOUR SURGEON IS BRILLIANT BUT I CAN'T LIE, HE'S ALSO A RAGING ALCOHOLIC, SO IT COULD GO EITHER WAY.

BUT WHAT IF I NEVER REGAIN MY POWERS? I HAD SUCH GREAT POWERS...

LIKE BEING ABLE TO FLY AT SUPERSONIC SPEEDS THROUGH SPACE AND FIXING THOSE CRAPPY ROCKETS THAT ELON MUSK MAKES WHICH ARE ALWAYS GOING WRONG

AND BEING ABLE TO SHOOT SONG LYRICS THROUGH THE AIR IN THE FORM OF NUCLEAR SOUNDWAVES, WHICH CAN DESTABILISE THE MOLECULAR STRUCTURES OF OBJECTS,

SO THAT A BLAST OF THE BEATLES' 'I AM THE WALRUS' PARTICULARLY THE LYRIC: 'YELLOW MATTER CUSTARD DRIPPNG FROM A DEAD DOG'S EYE,' SOFTENS UP THE METAL SKIN OF THE ROCKET, ALLOWING ME TO INSERT MY HAND

Lorem Iosum

AND REPAIR THE TOILET CISTERN WHICH, IS ALWAYS THE FIRST THING TO GO WRONG IN THESE JUNK ROCKETS.

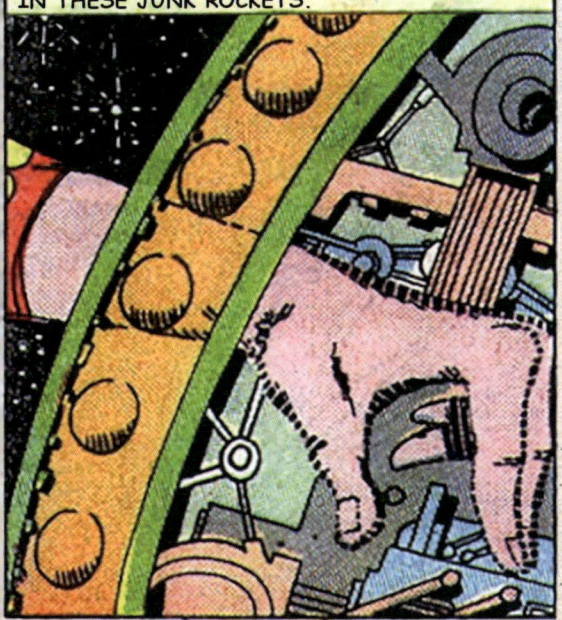

HOUSTON TO SCOTT, WE'RE LOVING THE BEATLES, BUT HOW ABOUT SOMETHING MORE CONTEMPORARY NEXT TIME?

I HAVE ANOTHER POWER WHERE I RUN REALLY FAST AT A SOLID OBJECT, LIKE A METAL WALL. IT LOOKS LIKE I'M GONNA BUST MY HEAD OPEN AND BLEED TO DEATH LIKE AN IDIOT. BUT I SPEED UP AND LEAP FORWARD.....

THEN, IN MID-AIR, I CHANGE MY ATOMIC STRUCTURE AND OVAL SHAPES REPRESENTING NUCLEAR ENERGY APPEAR ALL ROUND ME.

I TIGHTEN MY BUTT CHEEKS AND AS I HIT THE WALL IT SUDDENLY MELTS LIKE I'M DIVING INTO A CHEESE FONDUE, THEN I EMERGE ON THE OTHER SIDE...

AND CATCH THE BAD GUYS BURNING THE EVIDENCE...

HEY, DON'T YOU KNOCK BEFORE COMING INTO A ROOM? WHAT IF I'D BEEN DOING PILATES NAKED OR SOMETHING?

...THEN I'D JUST BEAT THE CRAP OUT THEM

SCOTT, YOU'RE SO MACHO AND YET SO SENSITIVE - A VERY SEXY COMBO. BUT WHAT HAPPENED TO YOUR INCREDIBLE POWERS?

I FOUGHT A SINISTER ROBOT AFTER EATING A BAD OYSTER...

SO YOU HAD A DODGY BOTTY DID YOU? IT'S OK YOU CAN TELL ME THINGS LIKE THAT, I'M A NURSE.

YES AND IT MEANT MY MUSICAL POWERS WERE WEAKENED. HERE'S A FLASH-BACK TO EXPLAIN...

WITH MY ABILITY TO PICK UP INFRA-DIG, OFF THE SPECTRUM SOUND WAVES, I DETECT AN EVIL METAL MOFO THREATENING THE EARTH. DANCE PRACTICE WILL HAVE TO WAIT!

I WAS FLOATING OVER THE VENUSIAN COUNTRYSIDE PRACTISING MY AERIAL DUCK DANCE WHICH INVOLVES WEBBING MY FINGERS OUT WHEN, IN THE DISTANCE, I SAW A MASSIVE, MANKY-LOOKING ROBOT.

61

I HARNESSED ALL MY GIGAWATTS OF LYRICAL POWER AND HIT THE METAL MONSTER WITH THE LYNRD SKYNRD VERSION OF 'SWEET HOME ALABAMA'. I HAD A NUCLEAR NERVOUS BREAKDOWN BUT IT WORKED! THE BEAST WAS VAPORISED!

SO AFTER SAVING MANKIND I'VE DISCOVERED THAT THE ONLY USEFUL REASON FOR COUNTRY AND WESTERN MUSIC TO EXIST IS FOR THE PURPOSE OF ELIMINATING EVIL ALIEN ROBOTS. THAT'S IT!

BUT SINGING ALL THOSE HOKEY, SENTIMENTAL, GOOD OL' BOY LYRICS HAD TAKEN THE LAST RESERVES OF MY ENERGY AND I COULD FEEL MY POWERS EBBING AWAY FASTER THAN A US PRESIDENT'S SANITY.

IS THIS THE END OF SCOTT GIGAWATT? WILL THERE BE A SECOND SERIES OR WILL I BE CANCELLED IN FAVOUR OF ANOTHER SHIT GAMESHOW HOSTED BY JIMMY CARR OR PADDY MCGUINNESS? READ ON TO FIND OUT.

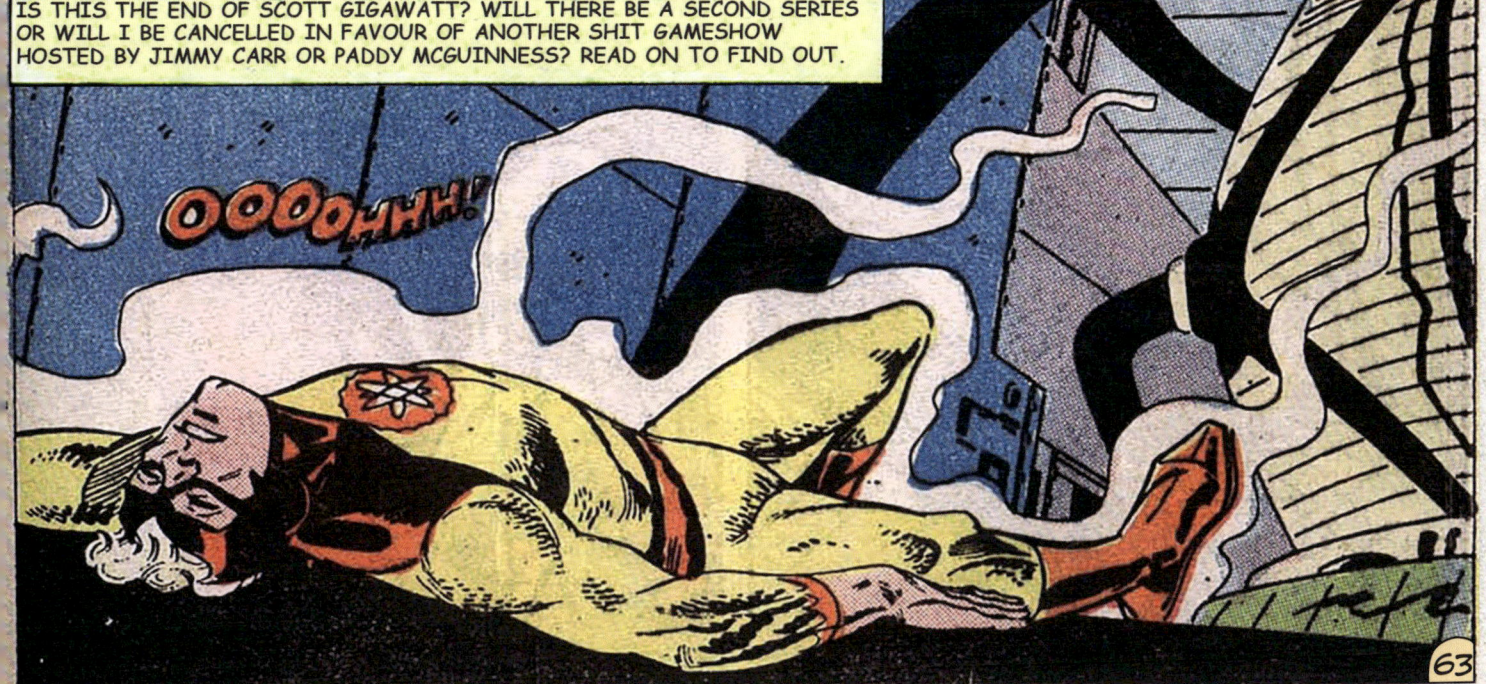

63

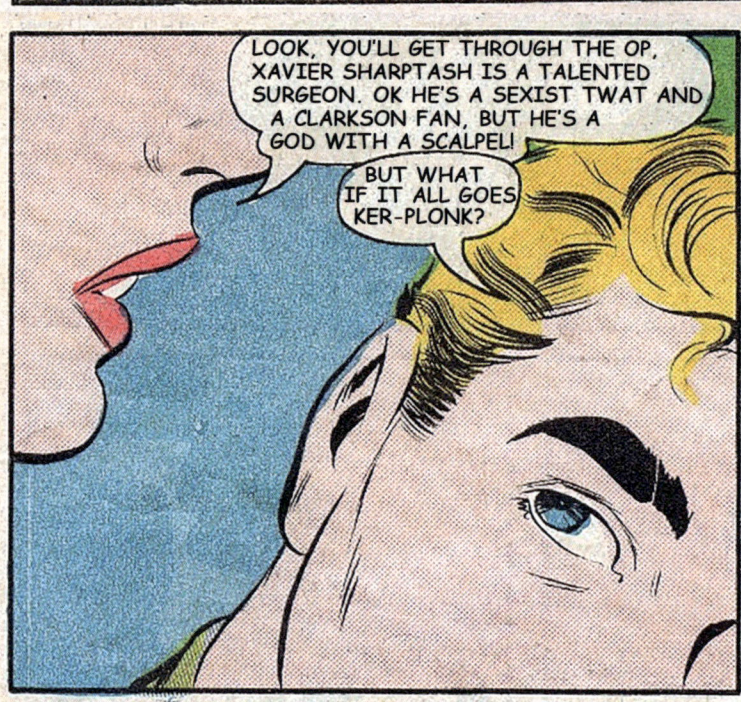

64

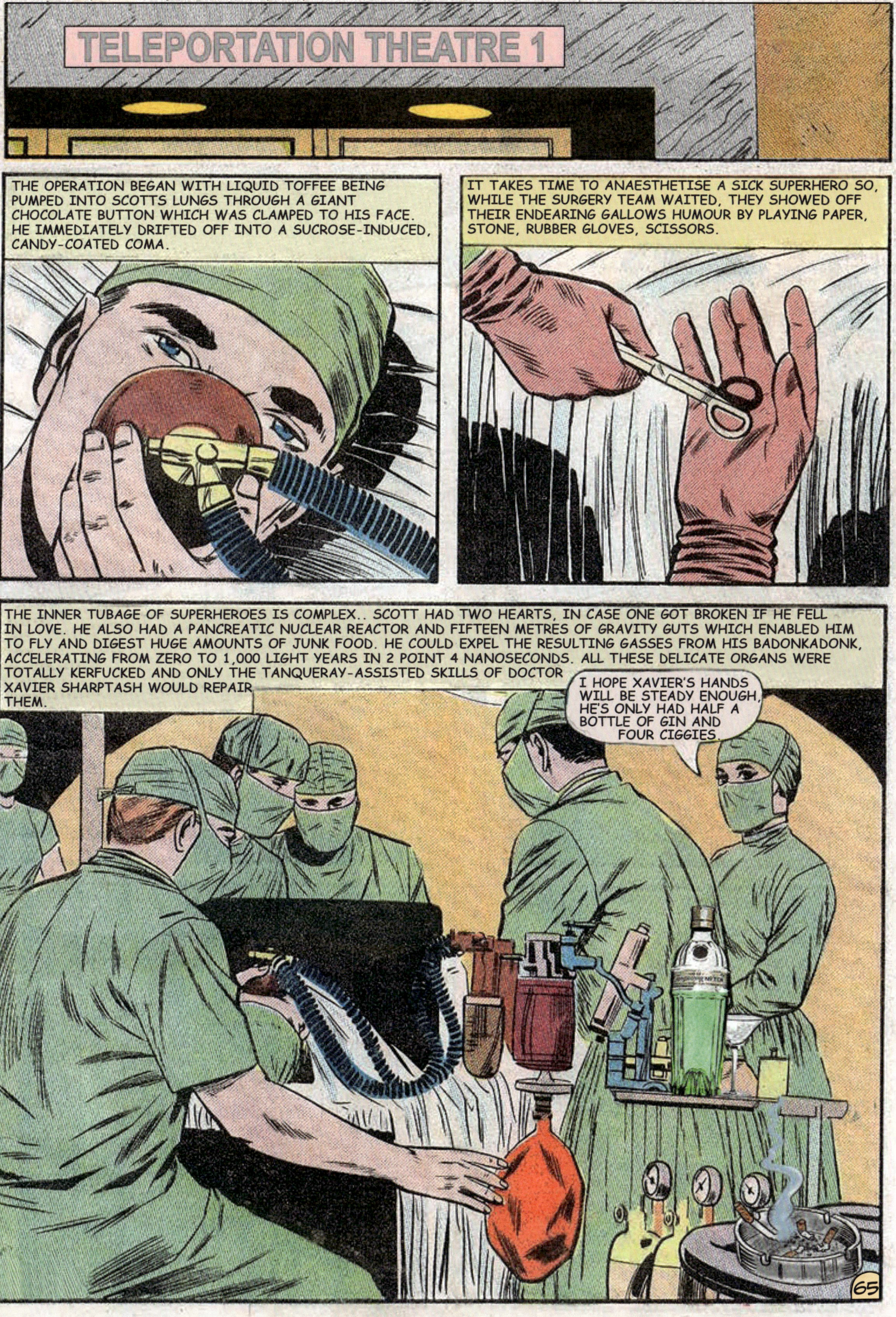

THE OPERATION BEGAN WITH LIQUID TOFFEE BEING PUMPED INTO SCOTTS LUNGS THROUGH A GIANT CHOCOLATE BUTTON WHICH WAS CLAMPED TO HIS FACE. HE IMMEDIATELY DRIFTED OFF INTO A SUCROSE-INDUCED, CANDY-COATED COMA.

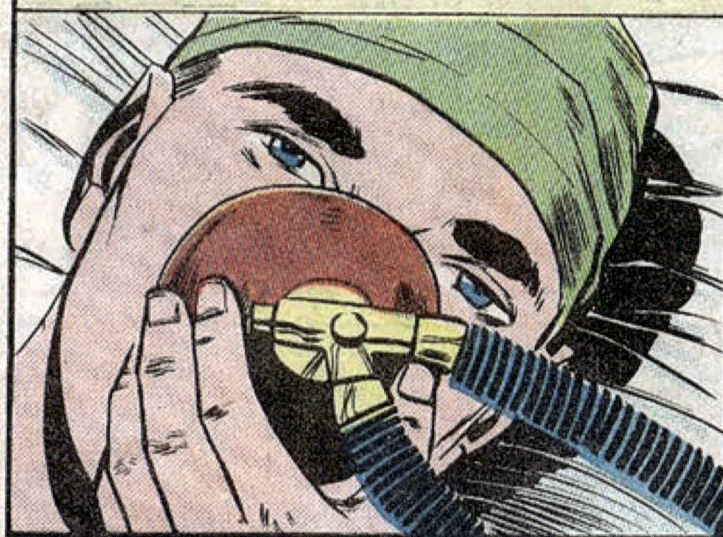

IT TAKES TIME TO ANAESTHETISE A SICK SUPERHERO SO, WHILE THE SURGERY TEAM WAITED, THEY SHOWED OFF THEIR ENDEARING GALLOWS HUMOUR BY PLAYING PAPER, STONE, RUBBER GLOVES, SCISSORS.

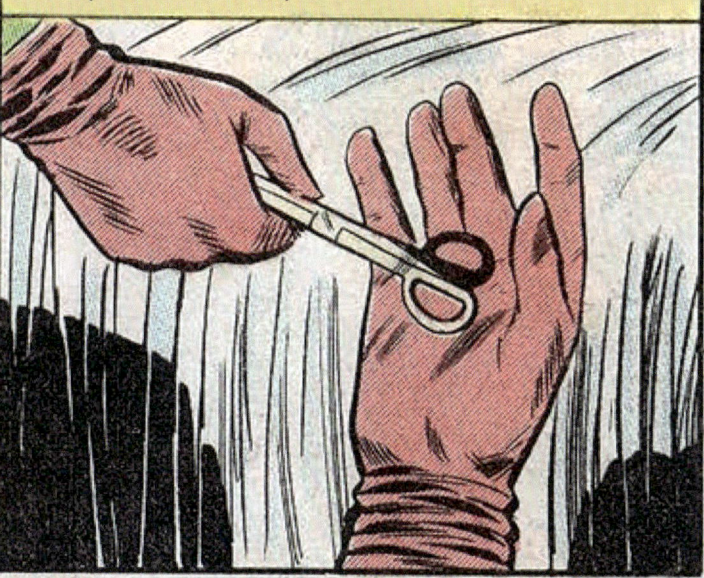

THE INNER TUBAGE OF SUPERHEROES IS COMPLEX.. SCOTT HAD TWO HEARTS, IN CASE ONE GOT BROKEN IF HE FELL IN LOVE. HE ALSO HAD A PANCREATIC NUCLEAR REACTOR AND FIFTEEN METRES OF GRAVITY GUTS WHICH ENABLED HIM TO FLY AND DIGEST HUGE AMOUNTS OF JUNK FOOD. HE COULD EXPEL THE RESULTING GASSES FROM HIS BADONKADONK, ACCELERATING FROM ZERO TO 1,000 LIGHT YEARS IN 2 POINT 4 NANOSECONDS. ALL THESE DELICATE ORGANS WERE TOTALLY KERFUCKED AND ONLY THE TANQUERAY-ASSISTED SKILLS OF DOCTOR XAVIER SHARPTASH WOULD REPAIR THEM.

I HOPE XAVIER'S HANDS WILL BE STEADY ENOUGH, HE'S ONLY HAD HALF A BOTTLE OF GIN AND FOUR CIGGIES

65

XAVIER HIT THE BOTTLE A BIT TOO HARD AND CUT THROUGH SCOTT'S EPIDIDDYDODDYDIDDLEYDERMIS. THEN, SUDDENLY, TARANTINO-ISH QUENTITIES OF BLOOD SPURTED ALL OVER THE THEATRE.

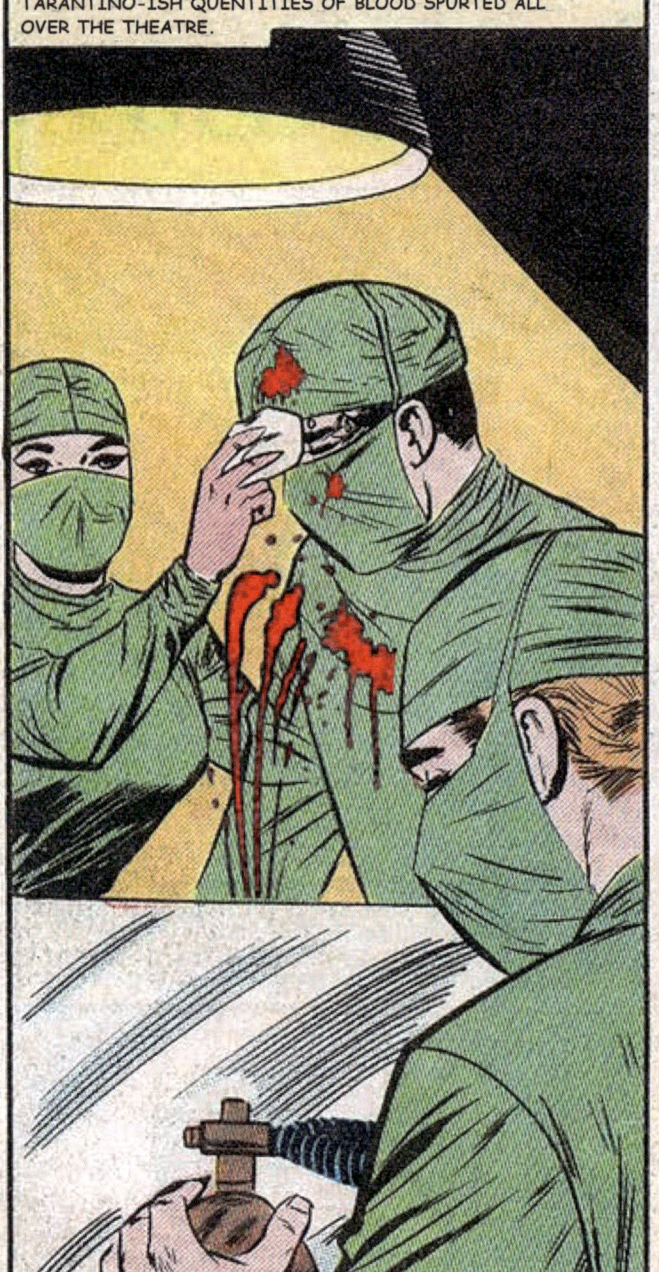

IT WAS TOUCH AND GO, HERE AND THERE, BY AND LARGE. THE LIGHTING WENT MOODY TO HEIGHTEN THE DRAMA AND SOMEONE PLAYED DISCORDANT PLINKY-PLONKY PIANO MUSIC. THE TEAM WERE IN EXTREME CLOSE UP AS THEY RUMMAGED AROUND IN THE BOWELS OF SCOTT'S BOWELS.

WITH A FEW TURNS OF A 25MM NUCLEAR SPANNER TO LOOSEN HIS FUSED COCCYX, SCOTT'S SUPERPOWERS STARTED TO COME BACK IN A TINY TRICKLE LIKE THE SPRING WATERS OF THE WORLD'S RIVERS AFTER GLOBAL WARMING HAS MELTED ALL THE SNOW. WHEREAS THAT WILL BE TRAGEDY, THIS WAS A MOMENT OF HOPE.

I'M RE-PRESSURISING HIS BLADDER-BOOSTER NUTSAC WITH HI-OCTANE FIZZ, SO HE'LL BE BACK IN ORBIT IN A NANO-JIFFY.

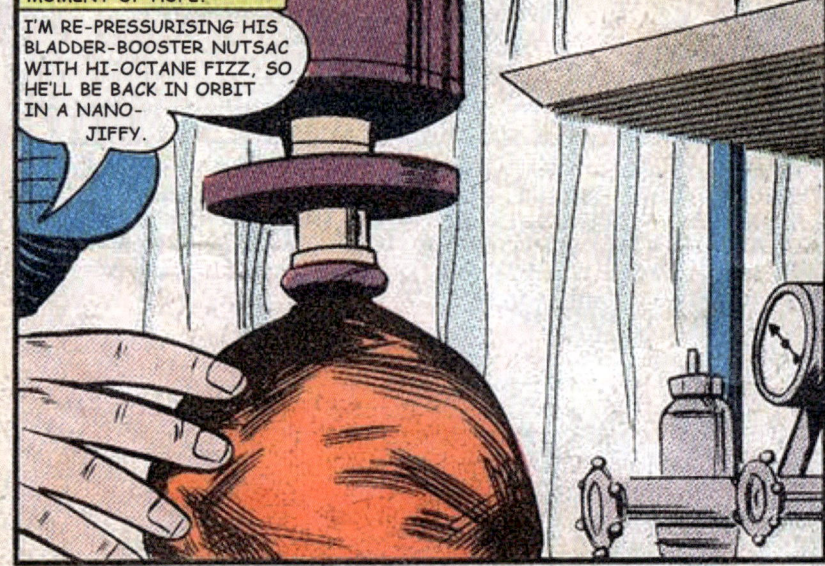

NOW THERE WAS AN ANXIOUS WAIT TO SEE IF SCOTT WOULD RECOVER ENOUGH TO CONTINUE HIS ONE-MAN STRUGGLE AGAINST THE FORCES OF OPPRESSION, OR WHETHER HE'D JUST ORDER A PIZZA MARGHERITA AND WATCH NETFLIX.

THE WAY YOU RE-ALIGNED HIS COLON WAS REALLY AMAZING! - LIKE WATCHING A TRUE ASS-ARTIST AT WORK!

THANKS FOR THAT, SERENA, I HAVE OTHER INTERESTS APART FROM SLICING PEOPLE UP. I'M A DUB POET AND I ALSO RUN A CAMPAIGN TO INTRODUCE SASHA DISTEL TO A GEN Z AUDIENCE.

I COLLECT VINTAGE SHOE INSOLES AND I GO EXTREME METAL DETECTING MOST WEEKENDS WITH JIMBO. - MAYBE YOU'D LIKE TO COME WITH?

SORRY XAVE, THIS WEEKEND I'LL BE BUSY STICKING HOT NEEDLES IN MY EYES.

NURSE, DID THE SURGERY WORK? AM I A SUPERHERO AGAIN OR JUST A RANDOM BLOKE?

I'M AFRAID IT ALL WENT A BIT PETE TONG. XAVIER WAS HASSELHOFFED. HE ACCIDENTALLY CUT YOUR CO-AXIAL PHONK-BEBOP-HARMONY INTERFACE PIPE. SO NOW, YOU'RE COMPLETELY TONE MUTT AND JEFF!

SUPERHERO A&E

HE ALSO DAMAGED ONE OF YOUR HEARTS AND PUNCTURED YOUR CRANIAL G-FORCE VALVE WHICH MEANS IF YOU FLY ABOVE AN ALTITUDE OF THREE FEET, YOU'LL HAVE A BRAIN SEIZURE AND START PLAYING PICKLEBALL..

AND THEN BANG ON ABOUT HOW BREXIT WAS A GREAT IDEA AND HOW BOORISH JOHNSON IS A GENIUS..

OMFG! MY LIFE IS OVER! I MIGHT AS WELL DIE OR ENTER CELEBRITY GET ME OUT OF HERE!!

ONLY JOKING, LOL!. IT WAS A SUCCESS! YOU CAN SLIP THAT SKIMPY, BODYSUIT BACK ON, BABE!

HA! YOU'RE SO FUNNY. IF YOU EVER NEED TO BE RESCUED FROM A BURNING ASTEROID, CALL ME!

67

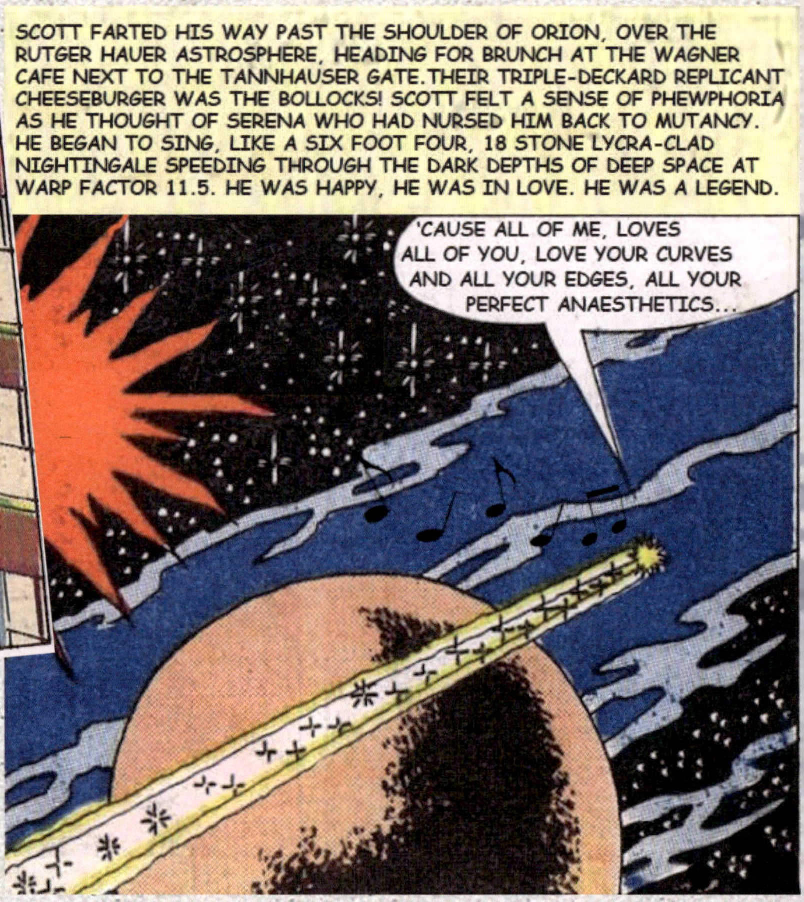

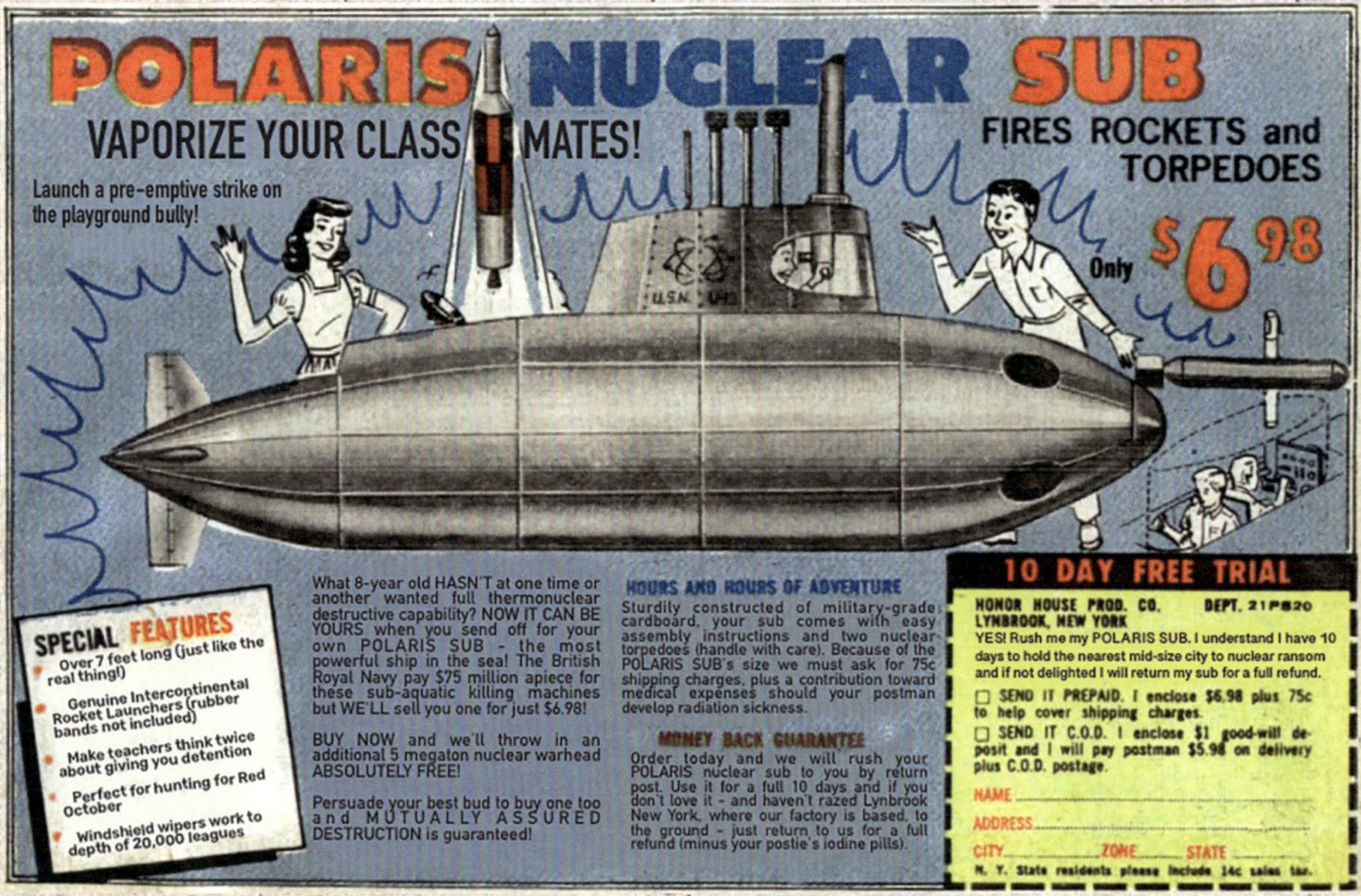

THE HONEYMOON OF HORROR VOL 1 Jan-Dec 2025 Published tetra-monthly by COMICS REBUBBLED CRIMINAL ENTERPRISES INC. EDITORIAL OFFICES 909 MADISON AVENUE, CRICKLEWOOD, NW2. Carmine Incognito: Publisher. Sue Doniym, Editor. Norm D. Plume, Production Manager. To advertise in this publication please leave a £20 note taped behind the cistern in the unisex toilet at the Cricklewood Harvester. Copyright Comics Rebubbled 2023. All rights reserved under international and Pan-Galactic Copyright Conventions. The stories, characters and incidents mentioned in this magazine are completely ludicrous and invented by total idiots. No actual persons, living or dead, should ever have to read this shit. But we've got your money now, so tough!

SIRI FELL IN LOVE WITH HER DIVORCE ATTORNEY, ALLY MONET – WHO PROMISED *THEIR* HONEYMOON WOULD BE *DIFFERENT*. AND IT WAS. IT WAS IN *EGHAM.*

SURPRISE! I *SAID* WE'D BE AT THE TRAVELODGE BUT IT'S ACTUALLY A TRAVELODGE *PLUS!*

IT HAS A LAVAZZA MACHINE *AND* BEDSIDE USB PORTS!

OH DARLING THAT'S *WONDERF--*WHO'S THAT IN THE DOORWAY?

WHERE?

THEY WERE RIGHT THERE, JUST A SECOND AGO. PERHAPS IT WAS THE *RECEPTIONIST.*

YOU SAW A *RECEPTIONIST?* AT A *TRAVELODGE?* WHAT ARE YOU – *NUTS??*

I MUST BE – I'VE MARRIED A MAN WHO DRIVES A *ROLLS ROYCE* YET HONEYMOONS AT *TRAVELODGE!*

TRAVELODGE *PLUS!* AND I SPENT MOST OF OUR HONEYMOON MONEY ON PETROL TO GET US HERE FROM *STAINES.*

SIRI WAS WORRIED SHE HAD MARRIED ALLY TOO *QUICKLY.* SHE'D ONLY FILED FOR *DIVORCE* FROM HUNTER LAST NIGHT BUT ALLY KNEW A *BENT REGISTRAR* WHO'D MARRY ANYONE WHO WOULD PAY HIS *GAS BILL* FOR A MONTH...

BESIDES, THERE'S *NO* PROBLEM THAT CAN'T BE SOLVED BY A GIANT PUBLIC *SNOG.*

IS THIS TOO IMPETUOUS OF US? I DON'T EVEN KNOW IF YOU LIKE BEING *PEGGED!*

GUESS WE'LL BOTH FIND OUT *TONIGHT!* BUT PLEASE DON'T FRET, MY DARLING...

...EVEN IF I DON'T, WE'LL STILL HAVE *BRITISH BAKEOFF* IN COMMON!

⑦⓪

ACTUALLY...THERE WAS, AS ALLY FOUND WHEN HE DISCOVERED HE'D BOOKED FOR THE WRONG MONTH AND THERE WERE *NO ROOMS* AVAILABLE TONIGHT. SO THEY JUMPED IN HIS ROLLER TO RACE TO THE *OTHER* NEAREST ECONOMY *CHAIN HOTEL*...

ALLY? THAT CAR -- IT'S *FOLLOWING* US..!

PREMIER INN *PLUS*, HUN - THERE'S A *NESPRESSO* MACHINE! COULD REALLY USE IT NOW, ACTUALLY...

MAYBE *HE* WANTS THE LAST ROOM AT THE PREMIER INN?

DRIVING THROUGH THIS *FOG* IS BLOODY TIRING!

ALLY DROVE LIKE HE MADE LOVE -- WITH ABSOLUTELY *NO* REGARD FOR THE RUBBER...

ALLY -- WATCH THE ROAD! HAIRPIN!! *HAIRPIN!!!*

DON'T HAVE A HAIRPIN - CAN'T YOU USE A *SCARF*?

JUST COS ROLLS-ROYCE MAKE AIRPLANE ENGINES...

...DOESN'T MEAN THEIR CARS CAN *FLY* --

...AS SIRI AND ALLY FOUND OUT! *MIRACULOUSLY*, AS THE ROLLS ROYCE HIT THE GROUND THEY WERE THROWN CLEAR OF THE *WRECKAGE*, BUT...

ALLY? ALLY, ARE YOU--?

ALLY...!!

CLUTCHING THE *LIFELESS BODY* OF HER BRAND NEW HUSBAND, SIRI KNEW NO AMOUNT OF *NESPRESSO PODS* OR *USB PORTS* COULD BRING ALLY BACK TO HER NOW...

I CAN'T BELIEVE MY *FIRST* HONEYMOON WAS THE *BEST* ONE!

71

SIRI SLIPPED INTO A VIVID *DREAM* IN WHICH POLITICIANS WERE MADE OF *CHOCOLATE* AND VOTERS JUST *ATE* THEM. THEN SHE WOKE, STARING UP TWO SETS OF HAIRY *NOSTRILS*

SHE'S AWAKE BUT STILL IN SHOCK *AND* SHE'S A WOMAN – SO TALK TO HER SLOWLY, USING ONLY EXTREMELY SHORT WORDS.

I WILL, *DR. BEARDY*

MRS MONET? I'M *SERGEANT CONSTABLE*. YOU JUST *SURVIVED* A *FATAL ACCIDENT*.

AND WHAT ABOUT ALLY, MY HUSBAND? IS HE..?

DEAD, MISS, HENCE *FATAL ACCIDENT*. WE BROUGHT YOU TO THE TRAVELODGE AS *TRAVELODGE DREAMER™* BEDS ARE GOOD FOR RECOVERY AND THERE'S A *USB* PORT TO CHARGE YOUR PHONE.

OR IPAD.

IT WAS ALL TOO MUCH. A HUSBAND WHO TRIED TO *ENTOMB* HER. ANOTHER ONE *DEAD*. IT HAD BEEN THE WORST YEAR OF HER LIFE AND IT WAS STILL ONLY *JANUARY!* SHE PLUGGED IN HER PHONE...

GUESS I NEED TO REINSTALL *TINDER*.

I'M SO SORRY MRS MONET. YOU'VE BEEN IN A COMA FOR THREE MONTHS AND...WELL, I'M AFRAID...YOUR DATA PACKAGE HAS *EXPIRED..!*

THE *SHOCK* OF LOSING HER DATA WAS SO PROFOUND THAT SIRI HAD TO BE *MEDICATED*...

I'LL GIVE HER SOME MOLLY TO CHEER HER UP. PLUS, IT WILL BE NICE HAVING SOMEONE TO *DANCE* WITH. YOU SHOULD GO, HER WEAK FEMALE MIND WILL *IMPLODE* IF YOU ASK HER ANY MORE *QUESTIONS*.

THAT SEEMS TOTALLY LEGIT.

BUT EVEN THE *DRUGS*, PLUS THE 950 SEPARATE *SPRINGS* IN THE TRAVELODGE DREAMER™ BED WEREN'T ENOUGH TO MAKE SIRI SLEEP THROUGH THE NIGHT...

SIRI...SIRI MONET...ARE YOU THERE? WHOOOOOOOOOOO!

ALLY? IS THAT...*ALLY???*

ALLY...IT CAN'T BE YOU. YOU'RE *DEAD*. THEY TOLD ME. GIVE ME A *SIGN* THAT IT'S YOU..!

IF YOU'VE BEEN INVOLVED IN AN ACCIDENT YOU MAY BE ENTITLED TO COMPENSATION..!

THE SPIRIT SURE *SOUNDED* LIKE A LAWYER...

SIRI GOT OUT OF BED AND, WITHOUT EVEN STOPPING FOR A *LAVAZZA*, SHE RUSHED OUT TO FIND THE SOURCE OF THE *MYSTERIOUS VOICE...*

CAN IT BE I'VE BEEN *GASLIT*? THAT ALLY'S *NOT DEAD*? I NEED ANSWERS - ANSWERS ONLY WIKIPEDIA OR A *GHOST* CAN PROVIDE...!

IN THE *GRAVEYARD* OPPOSITE THE TRAVELODGE PLUS, SHROUDED BY DARKNESS AND MIST, SOMETHING *STIRRED...*

I'D JUST LIKE TO GET THROUGH ONE HONEYMOON WITHOUT VISITING A GRAVEYARD...

IT'S *ME*, SIRI - I'M *HERE...*

A SHAMBOLIC *FIGURE* SHUFFLED TOWARD SIRI -- SHROUDED IN DARKNESS AND ENVELOPED IN TENDRILS OF GRAY DRABNESS.

IT *COULD* HAVE BEEN HER HUSBAND -- OR AT LEAST SOMEONE WITH IDENTICAL *FASHION SENSE...*

ALLY? IS IT YOU? SEND ME ANOTHER SIGN YOU'RE A LAWYER. AT LEAST BILL ME FOR *TALKING* TO YOU..!

EASY, HOTSHOT. I'M GONNA HAVE TO SEE YOUR FACE BEFORE I LET YOU CUP MY RIGHT BOOB IN Y--*OHHH*

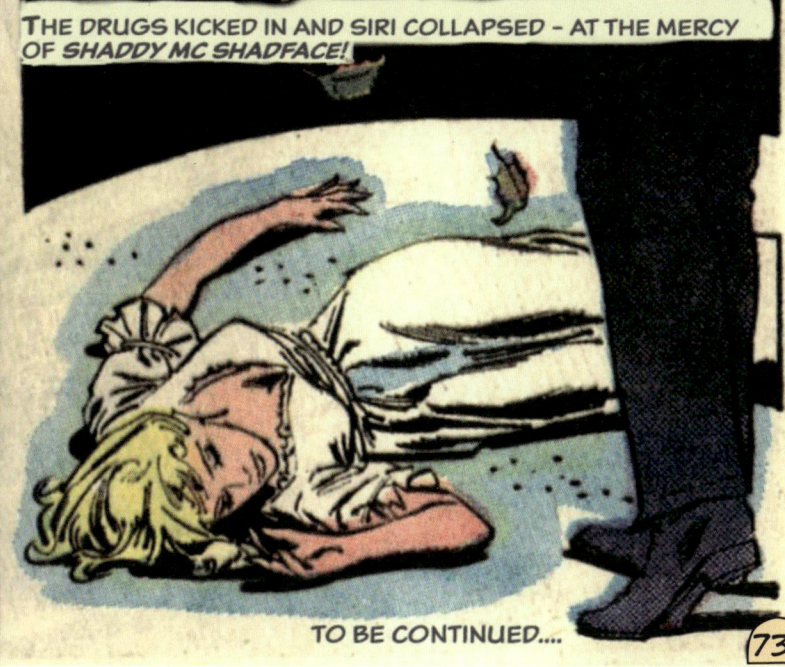

THE DRUGS KICKED IN AND SIRI COLLAPSED - AT THE MERCY OF *SHADDY MC SHADFACE!*

TO BE CONTINUED....

73

IN THE CASE OF...
"THE EGYPTIAN MINI-BREAK!"

CAIRO - CITY OF TRIANGULAR ARCHITECTURE AND LARGEST METROPOLIS IN THE ARAB WORLD! I WAS HERE INCOGNITO POSING AS A DELEGATE TO THE 12TH ANNUAL EGYPTIAN CONTACT LENS GRINDERS CONFERENCE TO CHECK-IN TO THE NEW CAIRO PREMIER INN. BUT THE MAITRE D' AT THE HOTEL'S BREWERS FAYRE RESTAURANT HAD RECOGNISED ME AND SEEN ME TURN MY NOSE UP AT HIS CHICKEN FORESTIÈRE - AND HE WANTED TO PREVENT ME FILING MY REPORT AT ALL COSTS..!

WOP!

YOUR FIST JUST MADE A RACIST NOISE AGAINST MY FACE!

WELL YOU'RE A DISGRACE TO THE TOMMY COOPER APPRECIATION SOCIETY!

WHY THE HELL DID YOU ORDER THE FORESTIÈRE? YOU DON'T EVEN LIKE DIANE SAUCE - INFIDEL!

YOU ARE A MISERABLE EXCUSE FOR A MAN! YOU *HATE* TRAVEL. HATE FLYING. DRIVING. DONKEYS. DECKCHAIRS. MINIATURE SHAMPOOS. COMPLIMENTARY BREAKFASTS. AND *FOREIGNERS!* I DON'T KNOW WHY *TRIP ADVISOR* EMPLOYS YOU!

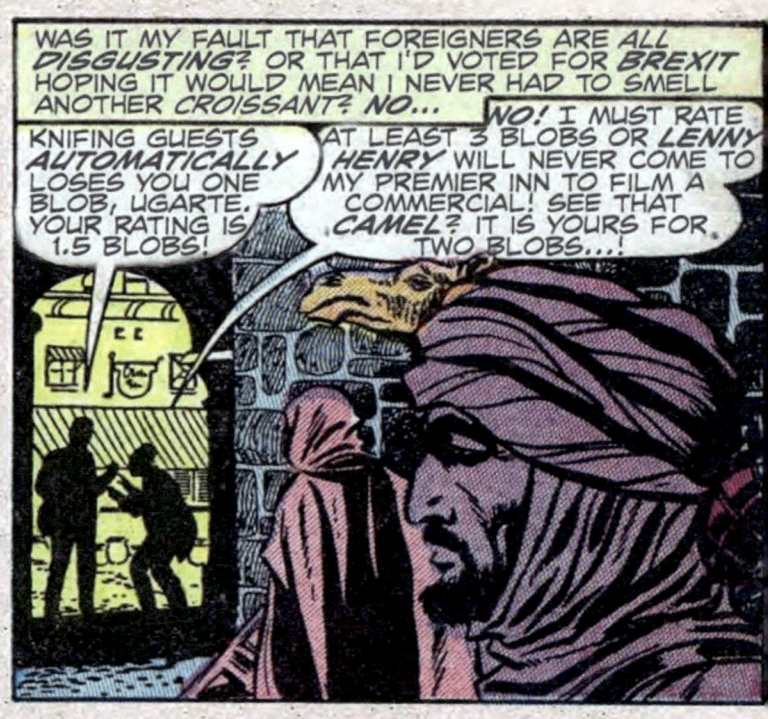

WAS IT MY FAULT THAT FOREIGNERS ARE *ALL DISGUSTING?* OR THAT I'D VOTED FOR *BREXIT* HOPING IT WOULD MEAN I NEVER HAD TO SMELL ANOTHER *CROISSANT? NO...*

KNIFING GUESTS *AUTOMATICALLY* LOSES YOU ONE BLOB, UGARTE. YOUR RATING IS 1.5 BLOBS!

NO! I MUST RATE AT LEAST 3 BLOBS OR *LENNY HENRY* WILL NEVER COME TO MY PREMIER INN TO FILM A COMMERCIAL! SEE THAT *CAMEL?* IT IS YOURS FOR TWO BLOBS...!

YOU CAN'T SWAY ME WITH A PAIR OF HUMPS AND SOME LONG EYELASHES, UGARTE. *OR* WITH A CAMEL. I HAVE A *DUTY.*

THEN LOOK AT *HIM!* SIX GUESTS JUST *VANISHED* FROM HIS AIRBNB, LEAVING JUST SHOES AND IDENTICAL 5-STAR REVIEWS!

IF SOMEONE WAS *KILLING* AIRBNB USERS, *TRIPADVISOR* WOULD WANNA KNOW - IF ONLY SO IT COULD FIND A WAY TO *ACCELERATE* THE PROCESS...

IF YOU'RE LYING TO ME...

IT IS TRUE! JUST LOOK AT THE INFIDEL IN HIS HAT WITH *NO PONYTAIL...!*

I TAILED THE GUY THRU THE *COPTIC QUARTER,* HOME TO MANY *CHRISTIAN* CHURCHES. NOT THAT HE WAS GOING THERE. HE PROBABLY COULDN'T FACE GOD...

...NOT AFTER MURDERING SIX TOURISTS. *NO* TOURIST DESERVES TO BE MURDERED. EXCEPT FOR *AMERICANS* WHO CAN'T PRONOUNCE 'LEICESTER SQUARE'. *THOSE* GUYS DESERVE ALL THEY GET..!

WHEN I GET TO THE AIRBNB, I THINK I'LL USE MY ALIAS - *JASON SMASHIN*, COCKY COCKNEY COIFFEUR -- THO' I'LL HAVE TO EXPLAIN WHY I CAN'T EVEN DYE MY *OWN* LOCKS WITHOUT LEAVING A GREEN RESIDUE ALL ROUND MY HAIRLINE.

THE GUY ENTERED A GRUNGY *AUBERGE* BETWEEN A COPTIC OPTICIAN AND A SARCOPHAGUS SHOWROOM

WOTCHER COCK, I NEED A GAWD'S TROOF OVER ME 'EAD AND 'EARD YOU MIGHT 'AVE A *BRIDE & GROOM* FREE!

I'M VERY SORRY, BUT I DON'T SPEAK *GUY RITCHIE..!*

SO I WROTE A TRANSLATION OF MY COLOURFUL COCKNEY ARGOT FOR THE STUPID *JAMES BLUNT...*

YOU CAN TAKE THE *NILE ROOM*, SO-CALLED FOR ITS UNMATCHED VIEWS OF THE RISING DAMP

OK, I-WAIT! WHAT'S THAT *ODOUR*? IT--IT SMELLS LIKE... A MILLION ANCHOVIES *FARTING!*

THE SUPERHOST TRIED TO REPLY BUT THE GODAWFUL *STENCH* CAUGHT HIM IN THE THROAT LIKE A *KARATE CHOP..!*

YOUR TOILET MUST BE BACKED UP TO THE VERY *BOWELS* OF *HELL...!*

THE *STINK* GOT THE BETTER OF ME BUT AS I COLLAPSED I HEARD A *FLUSH* -- AND SENSED A MONSTROUS *SHAPE* EMERGING FROM THE BOG!

I PASSED OUT, TO BE WAKENED BY *UGARTE*, WHO HAD STUFFED BOTH ENDS OF HIS MOUSTACHE UP HIS NOSTRILS TO KEEP OUT THE *SMELL...*

WHAT DID YOU *DO* TO THE TOILET? YOU *ANIMAL..!*

I DON'T USE NON-*U.K* TOILETS! ALL TRIPADVISOR EMPLOYEES WEAR *LADY TENA* PANTS 24/7.

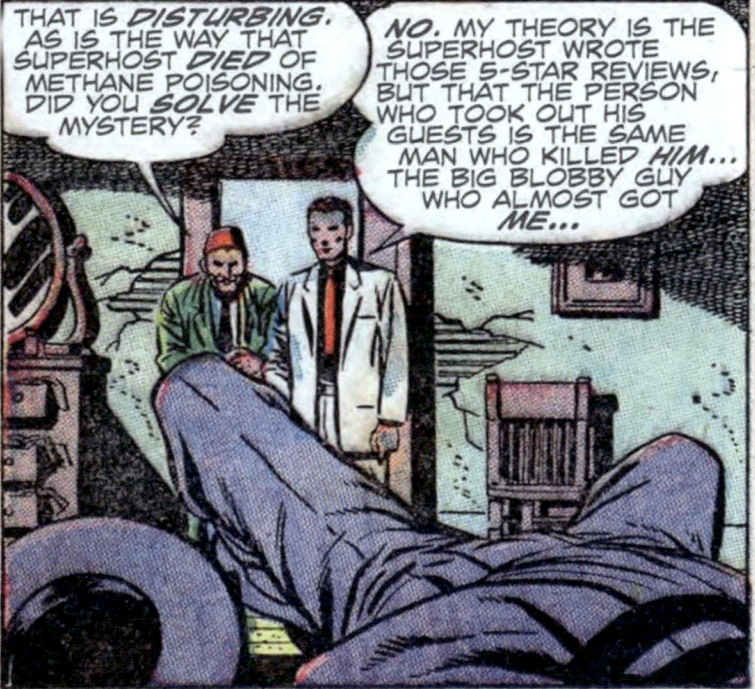

THAT IS *DISTURBING*. AS IS THE WAY THAT SUPERHOST *DIED* OF METHANE POISONING. DID YOU *SOLVE* THE MYSTERY?

NO. MY THEORY IS THE SUPERHOST WROTE THOSE 5-STAR REVIEWS, BUT THAT THE PERSON WHO TOOK OUT HIS GUESTS IS THE SAME MAN WHO KILLED *HIM...* THE BIG BLOBBY GUY WHO ALMOST GOT *ME...*

I HEADED BACK TO THE PREMIER INN, THROUGH THE COLOURFUL STREETS OF ONE OF AFRICA'S MOST *WALKABLE* CITIES...

...A ROUTE TAKING ME THROUGH THE AREA THE *HOLY FAMILY* STAYED IN 4 B.C, ALSO HOME TO THE COPTIC *ART MUSEUM*. THE WORLD'S A TRULY *INCREDIBLE* PLACE. WHAT A SHAME THERE ARE SO MANY *FOREIGNERS* IN IT...!

HELLO AGAIN, MR HAZARD. FORGIVE ME FOR LETTING MYSELF IN BUT I COULDN'T WAIT TO TRY THE COMPLIMENTARY FREEVIEW AND HYPNOS BED.

JUST SO LONG AS YOU DON'T HAVE TO USE THE TOILET!

SORRY ABOUT EARLIER. I HAVE IRRITABLE BOWEL SYNDROME, WHICH I'VE WEAPONIZED TO THREATEN HOTEL AND AIRBNB PLUMBING SYSTEMS. SO LONG AS THEY PAY, I STAY AWAY. YOU MAY CALL ME 'THE FAT MAN'

DO I HAVE TO? THAT'S SUCH A NEGATIVE STEREOTYPE!

INFURIATED BY HIS OPEN DISPLAY OF BODY-DYSMORPHIA, I SPRANG INTO ACTION....

YOU'RE JUST BIG-BONED!

I'M NOT SAYING HE WAS HEAVY OR ANYTHING...BUT HIS CHAIR JUST, LIKE, COLLAPSED -- ALLOWING ME TO GRAB HIS GUN AND...

ALRIGHT YOU SELF-BODY-SHAMING BASTARD! TELL ME WHAT HAPPENED TO THE TWO MISSING AIRBNB GUESTS AND MAYBE I'LL LET YOU SUCK ON A GAVISCON EXTRA!

THEY'RE MY ACCOMPLICES. THEY CHECK INTO HOTELS THEN LET ME IN TO BUGGER THE PLUMBING. RIGHT NOW THEY'RE IN BOGNOR, I SWEAR OR MY NAME ISN'T THE FAT MAN!

YOUR NAME ISN'T THE FAT MAN! NO-ONE'S NAME IS 'THE FAT MAN'! THAT'S LIKE HATE SPEECH!

THE, ER...MAN OFFERED TO PROVE HIS STORY BY GIVING HIS SECRET TRAVEL ITINERARY - PLUS REVIEWS OF EVERY HOTEL HE'D EVER STAYED IN - TO TRIPADVISOR...

C'MON. 'THE FAT MAN' ISN'T A NAME. WHAT DID YOUR MUM USED TO CALL YOU?

'THE FAT KID'. NOW, I LEFT THE DOCUMENTS BURIED UNDER A PURPLE PYRAMID. HOPE I CAN F--OH! THERE IT IS!

PROBABLY BE EASIER TO KEEP THIS SHIT IN ICLOUD...

I'M GONNA CALL YOU 'BRIAN'.

78

SURPRISE! THERE'S A *GUN* HERE TOO. TRY KEEPING ONE OF *THESE* ON ICLOUD! SEEMS WE ARE AT AN *IMPASSE*, MY TRIPADVISING FRIEND. DON'T YOU *LOVE* A MEXICAN STANDOFF?

I HATE *ALL* FOREIGN FOOD. WHY TRAVEL? ABROAD *SMELLS* - AND PEOPLE SPEAK ENGLISH LIKE ITS A SECOND FUCKING LANGUAGE!

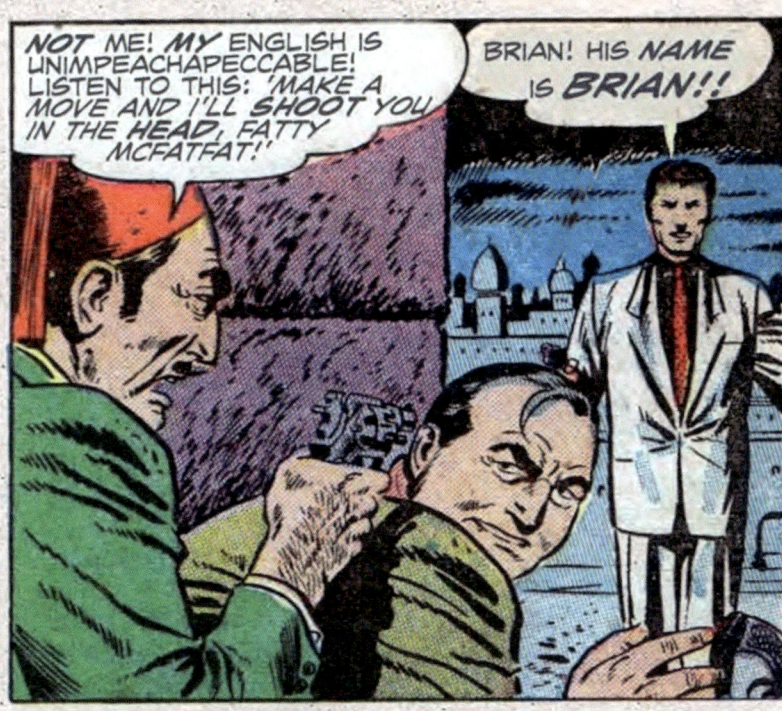

NOT ME! *MY* ENGLISH IS UNIMPEACHAPECCABLE! LISTEN TO THIS: 'MAKE A *MOVE* AND I'LL *SHOOT* YOU IN THE *HEAD*, FATTY MCFATFAT!'

BRIAN! HIS *NAME* IS *BRIAN!!*

NOW THAT MY FLUNKY HAS YOU WHERE I WANT YOU, HAND OVER THOSE PAPERS...

WELL PLAYED, CHIP HAZARD. I'D GIVE YOU *5 BLOBS!*

5 BLOBS? HE'S A *JOKE!* AND I'M *NOT* HIS FLUNKY. GIMME THE PAPERS AND DROP THE GUN!

I CAN'T FOLLOW THIS PLOT -- IT'S LIKE A CHRIS NOLAN MOVIE, EXCEPT THE DIALOGUE IS AUDIBLE.

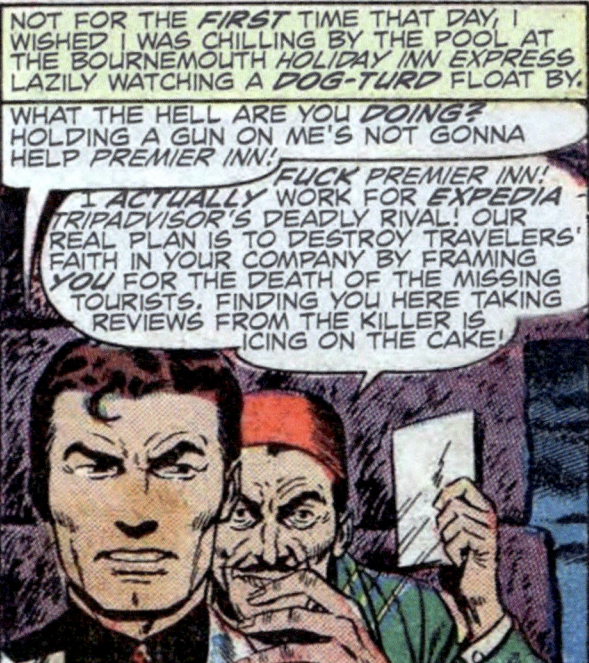

NOT FOR THE *FIRST* TIME THAT DAY, I WISHED I WAS CHILLING BY THE POOL AT THE BOURNEMOUTH *HOLIDAY INN* EXPRESS LAZILY WATCHING A *DOG-TURD* FLOAT BY.

WHAT THE HELL ARE YOU *DOING?* HOLDING A GUN ON ME'S NOT GONNA HELP *PREMIER INN!*

FUCK PREMIER INN! I *ACTUALLY* WORK FOR *EXPEDIA* - TRIPADVISOR'S DEADLY RIVAL! OUR REAL PLAN IS TO DESTROY TRAVELERS' FAITH IN YOUR COMPANY BY FRAMING *YOU* FOR THE DEATH OF THE MISSING TOURISTS. FINDING YOU HERE TAKING REVIEWS FROM THE KILLER IS ICING ON THE CAKE!

EXCEPT THEY'RE *NOT* TOURISTS AND THEY'RE NOT MISSING --THEY'RE HIS ACCOMPLICES AND THEY'RE STILL *ALIVE!*

WHAAT? THIS PLOTTING IS *SO* OBLIQUE! IT'S LIKE *GAME OF THRONES* WITHOUT THE TITS. OR LENA HEADEY...

I *LOVE* HER!

IT DOESN'T MATTER. I *STILL* HAVE YOU RED-HANDED BREAKING THE *NO TRESPASSING ON PURPLE PYRAMIDS* RULE AND COLLUDING WITH THIS *SHADY FAT BLOKE.* YOU AND YOUR OWL-OBSESSED FIRM ARE *FINISHED*, HAZARD!

ARE WE? OR HAVE I BEEN WEARING A *WIRE* THIS WHOLE TIME BECAUSE I'M ACTUALLY WORKING *WITH* PREMIER INN WHO *SUSPECTED* YOU WERE A MOLE AND WANTED YOU ON TAPE CONFESSING TO IT..???

OH FOR FUCK'S SAKE!

79

SUDDENLY, AND WITH SURPRISING SPEED FOR A --ER, FOR A *BRIAN*...

ARGH! MY *FEZ*...!

LIKE A CORNERED ANIMAL, UGARTE DREW A KNIFE! WAIT, THAT'S *NOT* LIKE AN ANIMAL. WELL, MAYBE A *CAT* -- CATS ARE *WANKERS*.

I'M TAKING THESE REVIEWS FOR EXPEDIA!

BRIAN - GRAB THE GUN!

UGARTE'S KNIFE *HIT* BRIAN! I HADN'T SEEN SUCH CARNAGE SINCE THE FATAL BRAWL OVER THE LAST *CHIPOLATA* AT LIVERPOOL *IBIS'S* ALL-YOU-CAN-EAT BREAKFAST BUFFET!

T-THIS SAYS *NOT TO BE REMOVED FROM BREWERS FAYRE*..!

I STILL TOOK IT! THAT'S HOW I ROLL AND NO ONE CAN STOP ME!

A FIST CAN! A FIST THAT WORKS IN *HOSPITALITY*!

THOK!

NON-RACIST SOUND EFFECT. *EXCELLENT!*

WE'D BETTER GET THIS KNIFE BACK TO THE *PREMIER INN* AND SEE IF THEY CAN SPARE A NAPKIN TO STAUNCH MY LOSS OF *BLOOD*. WELL DONE FOR EXPOSING UGARTE!

WELL DONE YOU FOR DISARMING HIM, YOU'RE QUITE A GUY - FOR AN EXCESSIVELY FLATULENT CONMAN.

PRAISE INDEED. BUT I'M NOT *REALLY* A CONMAN - I'M AN EXCESSIVELY FLATULENT *PRIVATE INVESTIGATOR*, HIRED BY EXPEDIA'S TOP BRASS TO *EXPOSE* AND DESTROY THE ROGUE CELL UGARTE WAS WORKING FOR! SO YOU SEE, ALL THIS TIME IT SEEMS WE ACTUALLY BOTH WANTED THE VERY SAME THING!

I ACTUALLY JUST WANTED SOMEONE TO EXPLAIN THIS FUCKING *PLOT*. BUT FIRST I HAD TO GET THAT KNIFE BACK TO THE *BREWERS FAYRE* BEFORE DINNER SERVICE...

CHIP, I'M GETTING TOO OLD FOR THE HOSTELRY INVESTIGATION GAME, THIS IS THE 16TH TIME I'VE BEEN STABBED BY A MAITRE D'. WHAT SAY WE BOTH RETIRE AND SET UP A *SOUS VIDE* CATERING COMPANY SUPPLYING FOOD TO REALLY CRAP HOTELS?

I TOLD BRIAN THAT SOUNDED VERY INTERESTING AND PROMISED I'D THINK ABOUT IT -- THEN GAVE HIM A FAKE TELEPHONE NUMBER AND GOT THE HELL OUT OF CAIRO. I MEAN, *NO OFFENCE*, BUT 'SOUS VIDE' SOUNDS FUCKING *FRENCH* TO ME...AND YOU ALREADY KNOW HOW I FEEL ABOUT *CROISSANTS*..!

THE END

A Dream of Rose's!

...SO ONCE YOU KNOW BILL GATES INVENTED 5G AS A WAY TO SPREAD **COVID** SO WE'D ALL HAVE TO GET INOCULATED WITH TRACKER MICROCHIPS, EVERYTHING STARTS TO MAKE SENSE...

OH CRAP - MY NEW HUSBAND IS A **DICKHEAD**!

FLEEING FROM A MESSY DIVORCE - MY LAWYER WAS INCONTINENT - I WAS HEADED FOR A FRESH START IN SPINSTERVILLE, ALABAMA.

BUT EVEN BEATING A NUN TO THE WINDOW SEAT HADN'T EASED THE PAIN OF ENDING MY MARRIAGE TO MY HIGH-SCHOOL SWEEHEART...

I MAYBE SHOULDA WAITED FOR HIM TO **FINISH** HIGH-SCHOOL BEFORE I MARRIED HIM...

OH WELL...YOU LIVE AND LEARN.

MAMA SAYS THE SECRET OF ROMANCE IS TO WIN A GOOD MAN, A STRONG MAN, A SEXY MAN - AND HOPE TO FUCK THEY NEVER FIND OUT ABOUT EACH OTHER. TO HELP ME GET BACK ON THE DATING SCENE MY NEW ROOMMATE **MADGE** HAD FIXED ME UP WITH HER BROTHER CHIP.

OH CHIP, YOU BOUGHT ME A ROSE BECAUSE MY NAME IS ROSE..!

AND BECAUSE I'M SO GLAD YOU'RE NOT CALLED 'BENTLEY'!

81

WISH I **WAS** CALLED BENTLEY.

OR FREDA.

OR TURDY MCSHITFACE.

OR **ANYTHING** TO ESCAPE THE WAY EVERY SAD FUCKER I EVER DATE HANDS ME A ROSE SO I HAVE TO PRETEND LIKE IT'S THE FIRST TIME ONE OF THE STUPID WANKERS HAS EVER DONE IT..!

SORRY, DID I SAY THAT OUT LOUD?

IT'S ALL GOOD. YOU AND I ARE THE DREAMWEAVERS OF OUR OWN TAPESTRIES.

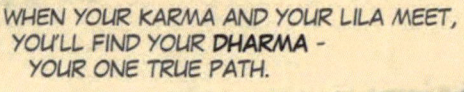

WHEN YOUR KARMA AND YOUR LILA MEET, YOU'LL FIND YOUR **DHARMA** - YOUR ONE TRUE PATH.

MADGE HAD WARNED ME CHIP WAS '**A BIT NEW-AGEY**' - BUT NOT THAT HE WAS GONNA CRAWL UP HIS OWN ARSE THEN SEND ME A SELFIE...

DO YOU TALK **BOLLOCKS** THE **WHOLE** TIME OR DO YOU JUST SAVE IT UP FOR **DATES**?

I AM IN A CONSTANT **DIALOGUE** WITH THE UNIVERSE - WHERE THERE IS **DISCONTINUITY**, COHERENCE CANNOT THRIVE...

AND THERE WAS MORE. **MUCH** MORE - CHIP TRULY PUT THE 'DUMB' INTO 'WISDOM'. I TOOK AS MUCH OF IT AS I COULD...BUT FINALLY--

SORRY! JUST REMEMBERED -- I LEFT THE IRON ON AND I'M A LESBIAN.

AND I WAS OUTTA THERE FASTER THAN A MEDIA C.E.O AFTER AN INDEPENDENT INTERNAL INVESTIGATION..!

82

CHIP RAN AFTER ME **BEGGING** ME TO LET HIM RECALIBRATE MY CHAKRAS, BUT I GOT BACK ON THE BUS WITH A BAD CASE OF **PTSD**...

PERPETUAL TOSSPOT SHITTY DATE SYNDROME. STILL, ONLY 39 STOPS TILL I'M HOME, THEN I CAN... **..OHHH NOOO..!**

I FORGOT TO BUY **BATTERIES** FOR MY VIBRATOR..!

AT WORK NEXT DAY AT '**WALLFLOWER, FRUMPISH & CATLADY REALTY**', MADGE GAVE UP TRYING TO FIND A BLOUSE THAT WENT WITH HER ORANGE HAT AND TRIED CHEERING ME UP INSTEAD...

SO SORRY ABOUT CHIP. HE **SWORE** HE WOULDN'T START TALKING ABOUT COSMIC LAW TILL **AFTER** HE SHAGGED YOU. I'VE TOLD HIM A ZILLION TIMES: 'YOU CAN WORSHIP THE DIVINE **OR** LOSE YOUR VIRGINITY - YOU CAN'T DO BOTH!'

IT'S OK. AS THE SAYING GOES, YOU GOTTA KISS A LOT OF FROGS IF YOU DOWNLOAD TINDER IN PARIS. GUESS I NEED TO GET BACK ON THE HORSE...

OH, YOU DON'T **NEED** A HORSE...

SITTING ON A WASHING MACHINE DURING SPIN-CYCLE WORKS EVEN **BETTER**! ALSO, MY COUSIN BO IS POSSIBLY HETERO-SEXUAL **AND** HE'S IN TOWN!

I MET UP WITH BO WHO INSISTED ON LIGHTING MY VAPE PEN AND TRIED TO CONVINCE ME HE WAS A FEMINIST...

THE PATRIARCHY HAS A LOT TO ANSWER FOR. I JUST READ A SURVEY WHICH REVEALED THAT **SEVEN** IN **TEN** WOMEN **REGULARLY** RECEIVE UNWELCOME SEXUAL COMMENTS IN PUBLIC...

WOW! THE OTHER THREE MUST BE **SO** UGLY...!

ROSE, I'D LIKE TO SHOW YOU MY MIATA.

DISAPPOINTINGLY, HE MEANT HIS **CAR** - THAT WAS OUR FIRST DATE...

WHICH LED TO A **SECOND** DATE...

THEN A **THIRD**. ON THE **FOURTH** DATE WE HAD A BREAKTHRU...

AND FIGURED OUT A WAY TO PUSH OUR FACES INTO EACH OTHER...

BUT THEN...

THE BASTARD SENT ME **ROSES**! DELIVERED BY DRONE TO MY FUCKING BEDROOM!

WHAT THE HELL IS INTERFLORA **PLAYING** AT?!?

MEN! THEY'RE ALL THE BLOODY SAME..!

WHEN THEY LOOK AT ME THEY DON'T SEE A LIVING, THINKING **WOMAN** - JUST A STUPID FLOWER-PUN!

84

I ELBOWED BO, WHICH **DEVASTATED** ME - I **ADORED** HIS **MIATA.** LUCKILY MADGE HAD ANOTHER COUSIN, **BARRY,** WHO TOOK ME SAILING IN HIS BIG FLOWERPOT WHICH IMMEDIATELY SANK

BUT THEN HE **RUINED** IT...

NOT **AGAIN**..!

I REALISED WHY A **ROSE** SYMBOLISES LOVE - COS TO GET IT YOU HAVE TO PUT UP WITH SO MANY ANNOYING PRICKS. I SWORE TO RENOUNCE MEN AND **SEX** FOREVER - EITHER BY JOINING A CONVENT OR BUYING ALL MY CLOTHES FROM **AMAZON BASICS.**

SHIT, NOW I'LL HAVE TO REJOIN PRIME...

AT THE **AMAZON** LOCKER NEXT DAY TO PICKUP MY NEW WELLINGTON BOOTS WITH ELASTICATED WAISTBAND, I FOUND SOMETHING **ELSE** TOO...

"ACCORDING TO YOUR PURCHASE HISTORY, YOU LIVE ALONE IN A TINY FLAT WITH A LARGE DIABETIC CAT, SO WE THOUGHT YOU MIGHT BE INTERESTED IN THE ENCLOSED INVITATION TO SPINSTERVILLE'S 100TH ANNUAL **SPINSTER'S BALL**..."

MMM...WONDER IF I CAN GET A SITTER FOR MR FLUFFLES?

AND READER, I DID...

HOPE THERE'LL BE SOME HOT MALE SPINSTERS THERE!

SPINSTE BALL

85

THERE WERE - BUT UNFORTUNATELY THEY'D PAIRED-OFF WITH ALL THE FEMALE SPINSTERS WHO HADN'T BEEN DRESSED BY AMAZON BASICS...

...UNTIL IT SEEMED I WAS THE ONLY ONE *NOT* HOOKED-UP

IN DESPERATION I BEGAN FLIRTING WITH A FOUR-EYED GIT WHO WAS *SO* HIDEOUS THAT HIS HAIRLINE HAD SPENT THE LAST FEW YEARS BACKING AWAY FROM HIS FACE...

I *NEVER* HAVE SEX ON A 1ST DATE UNLESS THE GUY IS WEARING A PAPER BAG WITH A PIC OF *CHRIS HEMSWORTH* PRINTED ON THE FRONT

SOUNDS PERFECTLY NORMAL -- YOU SUPPLY THE PAPER BAG AND I'M *IN*..! BY THE WAY, I SIMPLY *LOVE* YOUR DRESS..!

THANKS, THE WAIST IS ELASTICATED.

BUT WHEN I DISCOVERED I'D RUN OUT OF HEMSWORTH SHAGBAGS -- FOUR-EYES *DUMPED* ME!!!

WHY THE FUCK DID I COME? ALL MEN ARE *PIGS!* ESPECIALLY JEFE BEZOS...THOUGH I DO LIKE *MARVELOUS MRS MAISEL.*

I COULDN'T FACE THE *HUMILIATION* OF STAYING FOR THE KARAOKE, ESPECIALLY AS I'D FORGOTTEN THE CHOREOGRAPHY FOR *SINGLE LADIES* (PUT A RING ON IT)...

SO GOOD TO GET OUT OF SPINSTERVILLE, AND BACK TO A PLACE THAT MAKES ME FEEL GOOD, WHERE I CAN GET WHAT I NEED TO BE *HAPPY*..!

Nando's

AND YET EVEN AT MY REGULAR TABLE DRINKING A SMALL GLASS OF *PERI-PERI,* I STILL COULDN'T SHAKE OFF AN AWFUL, LOOMING AND INEFFABLE SENSE OF *FAILURE*...

THEN, ALL OF A SUDDEN....THERE HE WAS. HIM..!

BEM VINDO!

86

IT WAS **INGMAR**, MY EX-HUSBAND. WE STARED INTO EACH OTHER'S EYES, OLD EMOTIONS AND DESIRES **STIRRING**, UNTIL, FINALLY--

TEN-WING PLATTER WITH EXTRA CHEESY GARLIC BREAD?

INGMAR! I THOUGHT YOU WERE WORKING AT THE TRUMP CAMPAIGN CONSPIRACY GENERATION UNIT.

I WAS BUT **DONALD** SAID I WAS TOO NARCISSISTIC SO **NANDO'S** GAVE ME MY OLD JOB BACK. LUCKILY THE UNIFORM STILL FITS...AND MAKES ME LOOK LIKE A **GOD**..!

I...I'VE **MISSED** YOU. I THINK ABOUT YOU EVERY SINGLE DAY....

...AND ABOUT HILLARY CLINTON USING PIZZA RESTAURANTS TO OPERATE A NATIONWIDE CHILD-SEX RING.

INGMAR, IT CAN NEVER WORK. WE'RE TOO **DIFFERENT!** I'M A LIBRA AND YOU'RE BATSHIT CRAZY.

CRAZY FOR YOUR LOVIN' YOU MEAN..!

NO, I MEAN **MENTALLY UNHINGED.** YOU THINK YOU'RE GOD'S GIFT COS YOU CAN DO UP A BOW-TIE. BUT Q-ANON SENT BACK YOUR APPLICATION **UNOPENED** AND DAVID ICKE HAS BLOCKED YOU ON TWITTER TWICE. **DAVID ICKE!!!**

I'M LEAVING SPINSTERVILLE AND DOING WHAT I SHOULD HAVE DONE A LONG TIME AGO - MOVE TO **DENMARK**, WHERE A ROSE IS CALLED A 'BLOS' AND THERE ARE ONLY TWO BRANCHES OF INTERFLORA..!

AND I LEFT, PAUSING ONLY TO DRIVE OVER A PASSING ROSE-BUSH, CAUSING ME TO **CRASH** AND SPEND 6 MONTHS IN HOSPITAL WHERE I MET AND MARRIED MY PHYSICAL THERAPIST, **WAYNE**, WHO'S BEEN ALLERGIC TO ALL FORMS OF **POLLEN** SINCE BIRTH....

ISBN 978-1-7397120-1-3

9 781739 712013 >

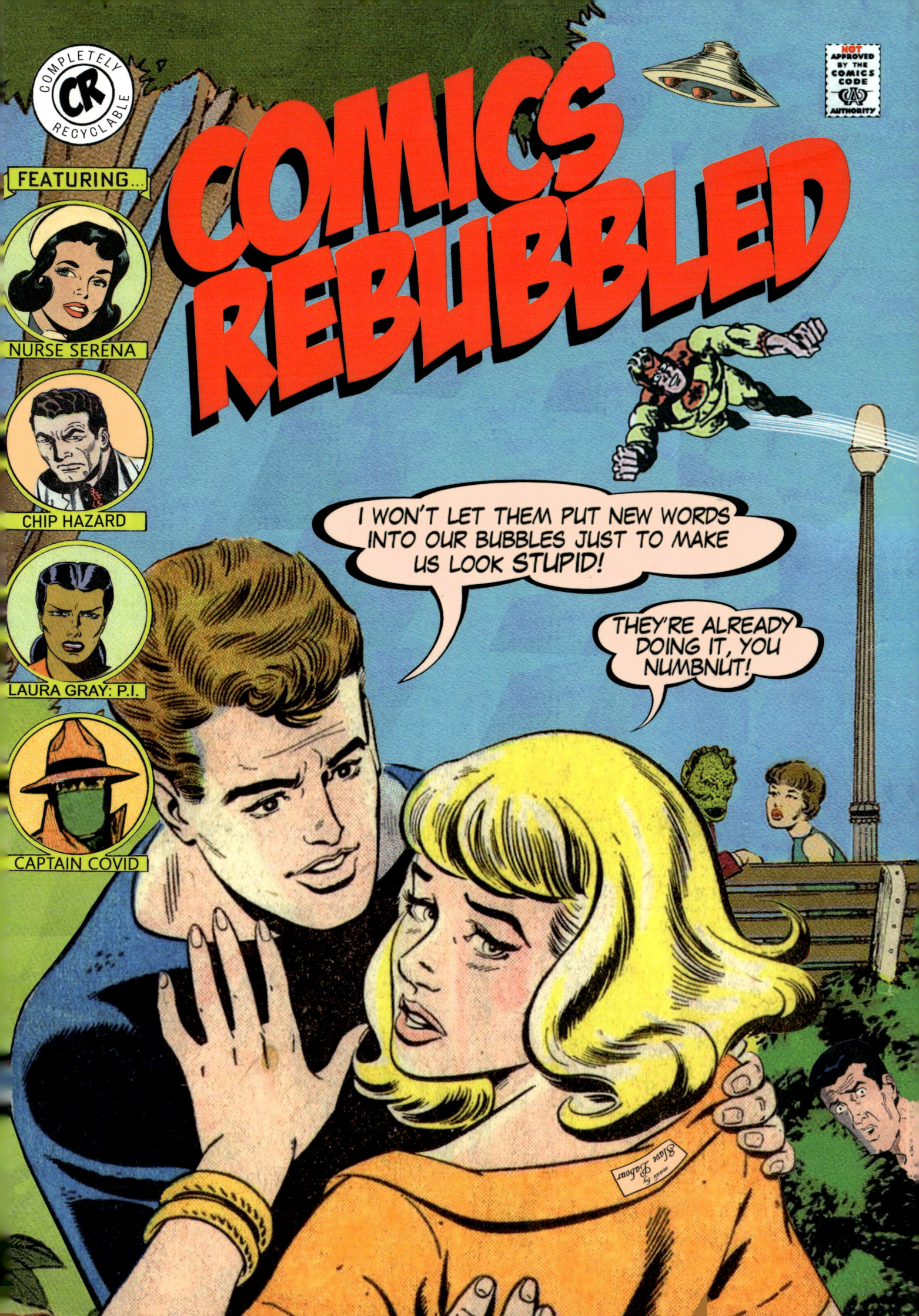